THE MONTEREY PENINSULA
AND
BIG SUR

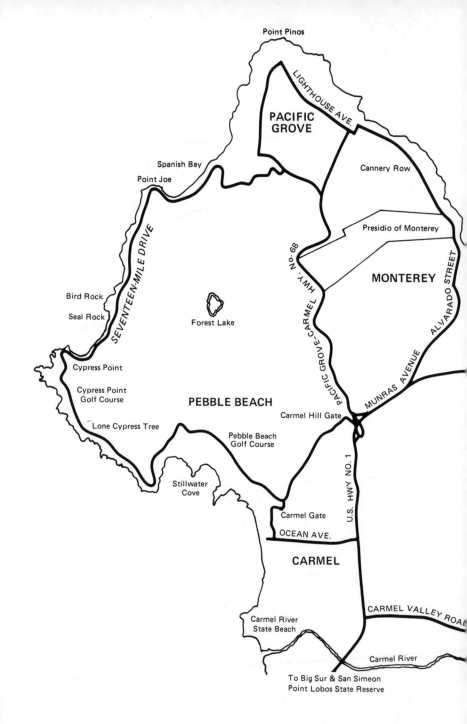

MAKING THE MOST
OF
THE MONTEREY PENINSULA
AND
BIG SUR

Maxine Knox and Mary Rodriguez

PRESIDIO PRESS
San Rafael, California & London, England

Published by Presidio Press of San Rafael, California, and
London, England, with editorial offices at 1114 Irwin Street,
San Rafael, California 94901

Library of Congress Cataloging in Publication Data

Knox, Maxine.
    Making the most of the Monterey Peninsula and
Big Sur.
    Edition of 1973 published under title: Exploring
Big Sur, Monterey, Carmel.
    Includes index.
    1. Monterey Peninsula, Calif.—Description and
travel—Guide-books. 2. Big Sur, Calif.—
Description and travel—Guide-books. I. Rodriquez,
Mary Dana, joint author. II. Title.
F868.M7K58 1979   917.94'76'045   78-11589
ISBN 0-89141-179-1

Photo credits as follows: Photos on pages 4, 11, 17, 21, 25, 50, 72, 88, 110,
courtesy of Monterey Peninsula Chamber of Commerce;
Photos on pages 30, 39, 43, 53, 142, courtesy of Pacific Grove
Chamber of Commerce; Photos on pages 74, 77, 80, 82, 94, 101, 116,
courtesy of Roy Nickerson; Photos on pages 56, 60, 68-9, courtesy of
Ron James; Photos pages 15, 19, 134, courtesy of Monterey Public
Library; Photos on pages 70, 97, courtesy of *Monterey Peninsula Herald;*
Photo on page 36, courtesy Jerry Lebeck.

Book design by Hal Lockwood

Cover design by Leslie Fuller

Printed in the United States of America

Contents

Introduction

▪ The **Monterey Peninsula/Big Sur** area has a special magic all its own. Rocky coastline, white sandy beaches, primeval forests, mist-shrouded mountains, crisp, smog-free air, and an historic and artistic atmosphere will make you want to return again and again. Each time you will discover something new and different to do and see. You can enjoy a restful holiday or a visit crammed with challenging activities and adventures, because there is something for everyone of every age and every interest.

Jutting out into the Pacific, the Monterey Peninsula is framed by the rolling ocean on two sides and the lulling waters of Monterey Bay on the other, with the forest greenery and majestic mountains of Big Sur completing the canvas. Located on the Central California Coast, it is 125 miles south of San Francisco and 345 miles north of Los Angeles and is easily accessible by car, bus or plane. Running through the Monterey Peninsula and connecting with major highways to the north, south and east is California's first designated **Scenic Highway, Highway 1** through Big Sur country. Interstate buses, an intracity bus service and charter bus and limousine tours are provided. Several scheduled airlines service the Peninsula, and private plane facilities are excellent.

The climate is pleasantly temperate. In winter months, when rainy days alternate with sun-filled weeks, the average temperature is 57°, and in summer 67°. Morning and evening fogs cool the coastline but disappear by midmorning. It is never really cold and seldom hot, nearly always sweater weather. You can golf, fish or play tennis during any month. Casual clothes are acceptable almost everywhere.

Because the Monterey Peninsula is so attractive to visitors and a popular choice for large conferences and small group meetings, it is well to plan ahead so you won't be confronted by *no vacancy* signs. This is particularly true in summer months and also during the time of special annual events, such as, the Bing Crosby National Pro-Am Golf Tournament, Laguna Seca Races and the Monterey Jazz Festival. For an uncrowded holiday, consider the fall and winter months when some motels have lower rates and check the listing of Extraspecial Events in the last chapter of this book. If you decide to attend one of these exciting happenings, reserve your tickets, if needed, and your accommodations well ahead of time.

The Monterey Peninsula is made up of several individualized communities: **Monterey, Pacific Grove, Pebble Beach, Carmel, Carmel Valley, Del Rey Oaks, Sand City, Seaside, Fort Ord** and **Marina.** Though of divergent origins, they complement each other and merge into a delightful area different from anywhere you have ever been.

Nearby **Castroville** and **Moss Landing** are entirely unlike in character from the Monterey Peninsula. Castroville is an agricultural community with emphasis on artichokes, while Moss Landing is marine- and antique-oriented. Each has its own particular personality, and visiting these two small towns is a rewarding experience.

By taking you along a simple route, this book will help you discover the special magic of the Monterey Peninsula area and Big Sur country on your own.

1.

Monterey,
the Old and the New

■ Monterey's existence and fortunes have been tied to the bay that shares its name since Juan Rodriguez Cabrillo, a Portuguese navigator in the service of Spain, first sighted it in 1542. Cabrillo noted this body of water in the ship's log but did not land on the tree-lined shore. The first visitor was the Basque explorer Sebastian Vizcaíno who named the area "Monterey" in honor of his sponsor, the Count of Monterrey, and took possession of it in the name of Philip III of Spain. Vizcaíno strongly recommended that the area be colonized as an outpost of the Spanish empire, but King Philip ignored him. It wasn't until nearly two centuries later, on a June morning in 1770, that Captain Gaspar de Portolá, Governor of Baja California, came by land with a small band of Spaniards, and Padre Junipero Serra, a Franciscan monk, arrived by sea. They met on the beach, raised a flag and claimed the area once again for Spain. Padre Serra set up the second Alta California Mission, while Captain Portolá, established the Presidio. Thus, the settlement of Monterey began with the cross and the sword as its symbols.

The Mission was later re-established at its present location in Carmel because Padre Serra wanted to remove his Indian neophytes to a quieter, more spiritual setting away from the rowdy Spanish soldiers in Monterey. The original Mission, the present-day San Carlos Cathedral, was known as the *Royal Presidio Chapel* and served the soldiers attached to the Presidio.

At first Monterey was only a fort. Five years after the establishment of the Presidio, soldiers' families settled and Monterey became a pueblo. With game plentiful, the forest thick with timber, the land fertile, water abundant, and temperatures moderate, the colony could not help but prosper. When Mexico obtained independence from Spain in 1821, Monterey served under a second flag as the capitol of Alta California at various times between the years of 1775 and 1846. The town was incorporated in 1850.

Monterey's geographical location makes it the hub of the Monterey Peninsula. Today it is a city of 28,000, deliberately uncommercial and with an aura of gentility which has led it to shun any form of air-polluting industry. Revenue is derived from the Peninsula's military installations, from institutions of higher learning, from a series of annual events and the scenic, artistic and historic atmosphere which makes Monterey attractive to travelers.

Live-oak-lined **Highway 1 (Cabrillo Highway)** leads into the Monterey Peninsula. When approaching Monterey, take the Fremont Street entrance. If you are coming from the north, stay in the right lane: there is a tricky spot where the left lane suddenly branches off without much warning, bypasses Monterey and goes south to Carmel.

Points of interest turn up immediately as you enter the city on Fremont Street. **Santa Catalina School**, in the woods to the left off Mark Thomas Drive, was founded in 1950 by the Order of Dominican Sisters as an exclusive girls' school, grades one through twelve. Now boys are also registered for preschool and grades one through three. The main building is an excellent example of Spanish-Colonial architecture revived. Though built in 1929 as a private residence, the methods employed were the same as those of early artisans who used no modern tools. Whitewashed stone slab walls, a red tiled roof and an abundance of wrought iron detailing make it reminiscent of early Monterey haciendas.

On the right of the highway is the **Naval Postgraduate School**. Here selected officers of the Navy, Marine Corps,

Hermann Hall, main building on the Naval Postgraduate School Campus

Army, Air Force and Coast Guard, as well as officers from twenty-two allied countries, are educated for leadership in the world of technology, science and management. The handsome old buildings with their tailored grounds and swan lake were once part of the most deluxe resort on the West Coast, and, even now, are often referred to as *the old Del Monte Hotel*. It was opened in 1880 by the redoubtable four San Francisco multimillionaires: Leland Stanford, Mark Hopkins, Collis P. Huntington and Charles Crocker. The elite of San Francisco and Southern California arrived in their private cars at the hotel's own railroad station, but Del Monte Hotel never quite lifted Monterey to the social eminence enjoyed by Newport and Saratoga on the Eastern seaboard.

When World War II created a dearth of help and patrons, the hotel was leased to the U.S. Navy in 1940 as a preflight training center. This famous old resort was closed as a hostelry in 1951 when the Government bought it and the surround-acreage as the location of the newly expanded Naval Postgraduate School. The buildings have been converted into administration offices, classrooms and living quarters for foreign students. All enjoy the elegant Roman plunge, tennis courts and acres of well-tended gardens where, in the early 1900s, millionaires and their ladies mingled with a new kind of West Coast society.

A left turn at Aguajito Road will lead to **Old Del Monte Golf Course** (public). Follow the directional signs to the oldest golf course west of the Mississippi, built in 1896 as part of Del Monte Hotel's guest facilities. The first tournament was held the following year and was so successful that it became an annual event which developed into the California State Amateur Championship.

Overlooking the intersection of Fremont and Aguajito on the tree-clad hillside is **Monterey Peninsula College.** This is a two-year, tuition-free community junior college with an average enrollment of 2,200 day students and 2,400 evening students.

A right turn off Fremont at Camino El Estero will take you along willow-fringed **Lake El Estero** where fat, spoiled coots and begging ducks make their home. Children love feeding them bread crusts and leftover picnic goodies. Ducks can nip fingers, so be wary. Pedal boats and canoes can be rented on the far side of the lake. On the shore across the bridge is a shady picnic area with tables and grills.

The **Visitors Information Center** is in the Armed Forces Y.M.C.A. building at the corner of Webster and Camino El Estero and is open every day from 9 A.M.–4-30 P.M. Here you can pick up free brochures and a guide to Monterey's *Path of History*, a self-guided tour of forty-six historic sites, which will make your visit even more pleasurable. An inexpensive street map of Peninsula cities would be a wise investment. The Monterey Peninsula Chamber of Commerce and its Visitors and Convention Bureau serves the entire Peninsula. The Chamber's headquarters are in the Rodriguez–Osio Adobe on Alvarado Street in downtown Monterey.

A number of helpful publications are available, free of charge, at many hotels, motels and restaurants. *This Month, Key Magazine* and *Village Gadabout* are monthly periodicals. *Monterey Peninsula Review* is a handy, weekly newspaper covering current goings-on. Other publications are also available: *Big Sur: A Guide; Guide to Carmel-by-the-Sea; The Gallery Tour of Carmel-by-the-Sea;* plus brochures distributed by the various Chambers of Commerce.

The **First Presidio**, older than the United States, was built by Costanoan Indian laborers on the site behind the Y.M.C.A. building. In recent years archaeologists have uncovered its adobe foundations and the fenced diggings have brought up many military and Indian artifacts.

Dennis the Menace Playground, designed by Hank Ketcham, Dennis' creator, and built by the Monterey Peninsula Junior Chamber of Commerce, is also at Lake El Estero, a certain stop if you have children along. Its landmark is a real, stationary Southern Pacific steam locomotive for scrambling over and pretend-engineering. There are several wading pools, unusual swings, slides and tunnels, and imaginative mazes, all free to enjoy.

Two blocks west at Pearl and Figueroa Streets is the **Monterey Tennis Center** at Jacks Ball Park with four night-lighted courts.

Returning to Fremont Street will facilitate sightseeing. Turn right on Church Street. In the next block you will see the original Mission founded by Padre Serra, now **San Carlos Cathedral**. This Registered National Historical Landmark is open to the public. Though small, it is a typical example of Spanish-Colonial architecture embellished with splendid Mexican folk art. This was the first **Presidio Chapel**, the most important church politically and religiously in California in the early 1800s, and was maintained by the Mexican Government. Building plans were drawn up by the Academy of San Carlos in Mexico City and are still on file in Mexico's National Archives. The **Royal Presidio Chapel** was completed in 1794 under the direction of Padre Fermin de Lasuen and the Mexican master stonemason, Manuel Ruiz, with the help of Indian laborers. Ruiz also directed construction of Carmel Mission. The Chapel was enlarged in 1858 when Monterey was a whaling port; so sections of whale vertebrae were used to pave the front sidewalks. The picturesque bell tower was added in 1893. In constant use since 1794, the church did not deteriorate as did other missions when they were abandoned after the devastating secularization of the missions in 1834. At that time many of the furnishings from the old Carmel Mission were brought to San Carlos Church. In 1850, when the Diocese of Monterey included all of California, the Royal Presidio Chapel became a Cathedral. Later the diocese was divided and the Chapel lost its high standing, but in 1968 once more it became a Cathedral.

An interesting sidelight about San Carlos Cathedral is that Lou Henry and Herbert Hoover were married by a Catholic priest in the front courtyard February 10, 1899. Both young people were Quakers, but since there was no Friends meetinghouse in the vicinity, Miss Henry's father, a prominent local banker, arranged with the bishop for a civil ceremony at San Carlos.

Behind the Cathedral is the trunk of the famous, old oak tree under which Mass was said when Vizcaíno landed in Monterey in 1602. Padre Serra, recognizing the site from Vizcaíno's description, offered Mass for the Portolá expedition under the same tree. Though badly damaged by lightning in 1840, the **Junipero Oak** still gave forth new shoots. When a utility company chopped it down and threw it into the bay in 1905, the dismayed chaplain had local fishermen retrieve it and place it in its present position.

You can sense more of Monterey's fascinating past along the **Path of History**. Following the orange-red line painted on the streets will take you to the most important historic sites in this cradle of California history. Some are private offices and residences, but many are open to the public; a few have gift or antique shops and restaurants. These authentically restored buildings are a credit to the members of the Monterey History and Art Association, who saved most of the original

Rear view of typical adobe

homes from destruction. Each spring the Association hosts an *Adobe House Tour*. Hostesses dressed in Spanish-Colonial costumes serve as guides. Maps for this self-guided driving or strolling tour along the Path of History are also available at the **Monterey History and Art Association** office in Casa Serrano, 412 Pacific Street, or at 550 Calle Principal at Custom House Plaza.

The Path of History can take a whole day, a half-day or an hour, depending on time available and whether you are driving, biking or walking along the 2.7 miles. A few of the highlights are described here.

There is a distinctive building design called *the Monterey style*, a reminder of Spanish and Mexican times, plus a little Johnny-come-lately influence. The term *adobe* refers to a house built of mud mixed with straw, which retained heat in winter and kept the sun's rays from penetrating in the summer. Whitewash (lime) was applied to the outside walls to

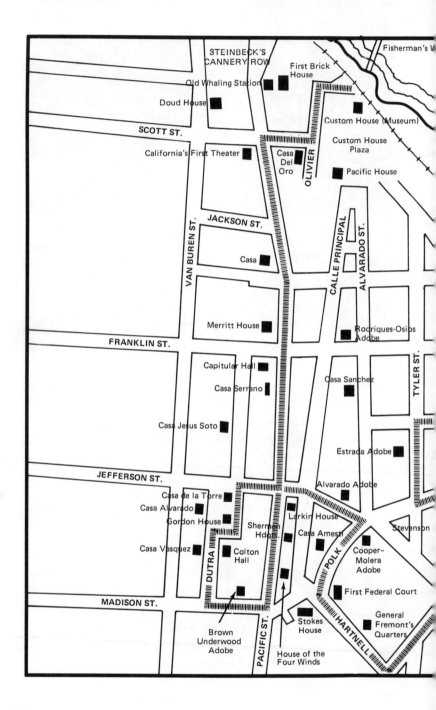

STEINBECK'S CANNERY ROW

Fisherman's W

First Brick House

Old Whaling Station

Doud House

Custom House (Museum)

SCOTT ST.

Custom House Plaza

California's First Theater

Casa Del Oro

OLIVIER

Pacific House

VAN BUREN ST.

JACKSON ST.

CALLE PRINCIPAL

ALVARADO ST.

Casa

Merritt House

Rodriques-Osios Adobe

FRANKLIN ST.

TYLER ST.

Capitular Hall

Casa Sanchez

Casa Serrano

Casa Jesus Soto

Estrada Adobe

JEFFERSON ST.

Alvarado Adobe

Casa de la Torre

Casa Alvarado

Larkin House

Gordon House

Sherman House

Stevenson

Casa Amesti

POLK

Casa Vasquez

DUTRA

Colton Hall

Cooper–Molera Adobe

First Federal Court

MADISON ST.

HARTNELL

General Fremont's Quarters

Brown Underwood Adobe

PACIFIC ST.

Stokes House

House of the Four Winds

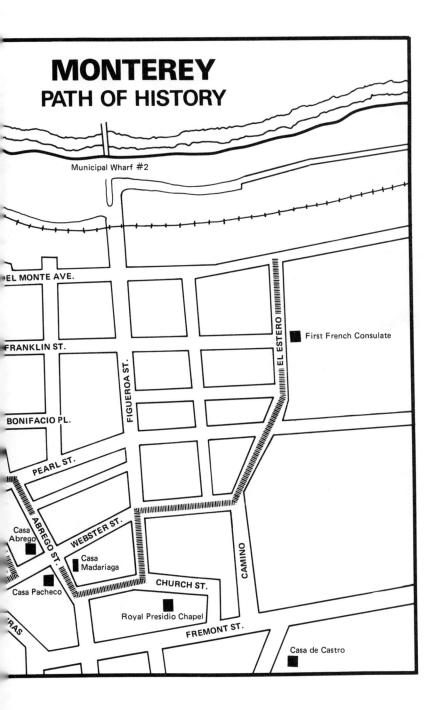

MONTEREY
PATH OF HISTORY

Municipal Wharf #2

EL MONTE AVE.

FRANKLIN ST.

FIGUEROA ST.

EL ESTERO

■ First French Consulate

BONIFACIO PL.

PEARL ST.

Casa Abrego ■

ABREGO ST.

WEBSTER ST.

Casa Madariaga ■

CAMINO

Casa Pacheco ■

CHURCH ST.

Royal Presidio Chapel ■

'RAS

FREMONT ST.

Casa de Castro ■

form a sort of plaster. Land was cheap; so a typical house was built with plenty of space around it, usually in the center of a courtyard, and constructed crosswise to the compass, letting the sun shine for some part of each day into every room. The house had two stories with living quarters downstairs and bedrooms upstairs. A balcony extended halfway or all the way around the upper story. In the Spanish–Mexican period, stairs to the bedrooms were usually outside. Although it is said this encouraged elopements, such a design had its practical aspects. The returning master could clean up without tracking dirt through the ground floor rooms, and he could also sneak in and out unsuspected if circumstances necessitated. New England influence later placed the stairs on the inside.

Some early Yankee settlers were ships' carpenters who built their homes of the pine and redwood, so plentiful in the area. Dirt and tiled floors were replaced with wood, and shutters were put on the outside rather than inside. The custom of building outside doors in pairs, with each single door too small for a person to pass through, was continued. There was wisdom in this since it was a good protective device. Eventually, the practical New Englanders replaced Monterey's bougainvillea-draped adobe walls and tile copings with white picket fences.

Many interesting Path of History sites are clustered in and around downtown Monterey. One is **Stevenson House** on Houston Street, which was owned by Jules Simoneau. **Robert Louis Stevenson** rented a room here, in the autumn of 1879, while courting his future wife, Fanny Van de Grift Osbourne, ten years his senior and the divorced mother of two children. She was visiting her sister and escaping from her unhappy first marriage. Stevenson House, now a State Historical Landmark, is an outstanding example of an adobe dwelling. Its rooms are filled with accurate furnishings and bric-a-brac of the nineteenth century and the largest collection of Stevenson memorabilia in the United States. Youngsters will be fascinated by the Simoneau children's room because it contains

Children's Room, Stevenson House, Monterey

small-sized period clothing and antique toys. The house is intriguing, also, because it has an alleged ghost or two. Sometimes the shadowy, romantic figure of Robert Louis Stevenson himself has appeared in the room he occupied. Another figure is said to be Mrs. Simoneau, who has been seen standing at the top of the stairway.

Pleasant **Jules Simoneau Plaza** with fountains, flowers, and benches is at the corner of Tyler and Munras. Not only was Simoneau Stevenson's landlord, but he was an encouraging friend who provided the destitute young writer with free meals at his restaurant and saloon which stood on this spot.

Munras Avenue leads into Alvarado Street (one-way), **Monterey's downtown business district.** After you have visited the many stores here, for further shopping you might try **Del Monte Shopping Center,** off Highway 1 traveling south.

The pretty, brick-paved, tree-bordered semi-mall at the

west end of Alvarado Street leads to the **Monterey Conference Center** and **Custom House Plaza.** The main offices of
the **Monterey Peninsula Chamber of Commerce** are in the
Rodriguez–Osio Adobe, 380 Alvarado, one of the earliest
stores which has since served as a residential and commercial
building.

Monterey's Conference Center has a 20,000 sq. ft. exhibition hall, 11,000 sq. ft. ballroom, 500-seat forum and addi-
tional small meeting rooms. In addition to being a convention
facility, the Center is used for social and cultural events.

A 6'7", 1,400 lb. bronze statue of Don Gaspar de Portolá proudly surveys Portola Plaza at the Conference Center.
This Bicentennial gift from Juan Carlos I was created in the
Spanish Province of Lerida, Portolá's birthplace. Coincidentally, this is how a nearby street happened to be named after
the King of Spain.

Calle Principal runs parallel with Alvarado Street. **Allen
Knight Maritime Museum,** 550 Calle Principal, reflects Monterey's nautical past. This museum was named after a former
mayor of Carmel who collected many of its exhibits during
his lifetime. Monterey Bay's history is well-represented in
three exhibit rooms. Admission is free. Hours are 1–4 P.M.
weekdays and 2–4 P.M. Saturdays and Sundays; closed Mondays and holidays.

Larkin House, the first recorded two-story adobe in Monterey, built in 1835, is around the corner at the intersection
of Munras and Jefferson. This building served as the American Consulate in Alta California when Thomas O. Larkin was
U.S. Consul at the Port of Monterey. The parlor is considered
one of the 100 most beautiful rooms in America.

Monterey's famous landmark, **Colton Hall,** dominates the
area between Jefferson and Madison on Pacific Street. In its
day it was the most pretentious building in California and
still is one of the state's most distinguished edifices. Colton
Hall was constructed with soft, yellow-white sedimentary
rock called *chalk rock* or *Carmel stone*, which came from a
quarry just outside of town. This rock was also used for most

Colton Hall, birthplace of California's statehood

of the foundations of adobe homes and for garden walls in Monterey. Walter Colton, first alcalde (mayor) of Monterey, was responsible for the first newspaper published in the state, the first school and the first library. He came here as a Congregational chaplain aboard Commodore Sloat's frigate *Congress* and stayed on to govern the citizenry. There is an excellent free museum on the second floor of Colton Hall, open daily 10 A.M.–5 P.M. Monterey's city offices are on the first floor.

Monterey Peninsula Museum of Art, across the street, is fully accredited with the American Association of Museums and has a prestigious permanent collection of art, including a room of folk art upstairs. There is also a book and gift shop. The yearly calendar of events includes selective one-man shows, exhibits, slide shows, lectures and art classes. Admittance to the museum is free. Hours are 10 A.M.–4 P.M. Tuesday through Friday; 1–4 P.M. Saturday and Sunday; closed Mondays and holidays.

Two blocks up the hill at 440 Van Buren Street is **Monterey Institute of Foreign Studies**. Some of the classrooms are housed in the old Carnegie Library, the first in Monterey. The Institute is an independent, fully accredited, upper division college and graduate school with a predominantly foreign-born and foreign-educated faculty. This is the only educational facility in the country completely committed to preparing students for positions as foreign service officers for the State Department, for work in the foreign service of other countries, and for preparing them in areas like multinational corporate management.

Perry House, a charming Victorian with a spectacular view of Monterey Bay, is at the corner of Van Buren and Scott Streets. Manuel Perry, a whaling captain, built this home in 1860.

Mayo Hayes O'Donnell Library, in the middle of the next block on Van Buren, was Monterey's first Protestant church. This century-old chapel was originally built on Pacific Street by the congregation of St. James Episcopal Church. When urban renewal threatened, the Monterey History and Art Association intervened and saved it by having the building moved to this site. It may surprise you to see a red church. Protestants painted their churches white in New England, but Californians always preferred red for their classic, little Gothic churches. The library's collection is concentrated on Californiana. The mellowed wooden floors are covered with Oriental scatter rugs; the period furnishings fit with their setting; and display cases hold antique buttons and fans, old quilts and other cherished items from Monterey's early days. The library is open Wednesdays and Saturdays 1–4 P.M.

California's First Theatre, a museum by day and a theatre by night, is a block down Scott Street at the corner of Pacific. In the middle of the nineteenth century, this was a saloon and sailors' boardinghouse operated by Jack Swan. In 1847 a small group of soldiers from the Presidio volunteered to

The lobby of California's first theatre

present two minstrel shows, and Swan's bar became the first building on the Pacific Coast in which paid dramatic performances were staged. Now the Gold Coast Troupers present live old-time melodramas Wednesday through Sunday evenings in the summer months and Fridays and Saturdays during the winter. The box office is open summer afternoons so you can reserve tickets. Sip "sassparilla," hiss the villain and cheer the hero. It's all-around good family entertainment.

The long, two-story adobe down Scott Street with the characteristic balcony on four sides is **Pacific House**, a former hotel and saloon for seafarers. The house and grounds cover one-third of a city block. There was a bull-and-bear pit here during Spanish and Mexican days; today, it is **Memory Garden** where Monterey celebrates her birthday with a *Merienda* (fiesta) each June. The lower floor is a public museum of Monterey lore, open 9 A.M.–5 P.M. daily.

The **Old Whaling Station** on short Decatur Street nearby was built as a private residence in 1855 and later became a boardinghouse for a group of Portuguese whalers. These men formed the Monterey Whaling Company and devised improved methods for harpooning humpback and California gray whales. Vessels totaling 640 moved between the California coast and the Hawaiian Islands. Some of the harpooners were South Seas natives with painted bodies and scanty, colorful dress who shocked local residents with their partial nudity. Whalebone fences were common, and the sidewalk in front of the Old Whaling Station is made from whalebones, as is the mantle over the entrance to California's First Theatre. The price of whale oil declined and whalebone use was limited; by 1877 the Pacific Coast whaling fleet was reduced to forty ships. Since 1937 gray whales have been protected by international agreement. They still ply their passage along the coast on annual trips to Mexican waters in winter, returning north along the same route in spring.

In the **Custom House Plaza** you can wander through expanses of red-roofed, white adobes surrounded by seasonal flowers. Plane trees provide shade and a Spanish fountain, a lyrical note. Adjacent to the Plaza is a bocci (pronounced *bott-chee*) ball court where retired Sicilian fishermen play their national game which resembles outdoor bowling.

Close by Custom House, near the entrance to Fisherman's Wharf, is a handsome bust of Pietro Ferrante, one of the three pioneers who founded Monterey's fishing and canning industry. Ferrante was awarded the Italian Congressional Star for the generous assistance he gave to other Italian immigrants who settled in this country.

The **Custom House** was built by the Mexican Government in 1814 and is the oldest government building west of the Rockies. This is where, in 1846 during the war with Mexico, Commodore John Drake Sloat raised the American flag, claiming all of Alta California for the United States. This famous adobe has exhibits from three periods of California's history when Monterey was the capitol. Four flags fly over the Plaza: Spanish, Mexican, American and California's Bear Flag. Many special events are held here, including the *Re-Enactment of Sloat's Landing* each July.

The entrance to **Fisherman's Wharf** is next to the Custom House. Summer days and sunny weekends you will be greeted by the organ grinder and his affectionate monkey. Much

The Old Custom House

Fisherman's Wharf, Monterey

of the activity on this pier centers around the wholesale and retail fish business. Two of the markets have been operating since the 1930s. Tourist attractions on the wharf are geared to family fun. Sandwiched between fish markets, boat sales, rentals and excursion concessions are restaurants, gift shops and bazaars, art galleries, candy shops and a book store. The many-colored buildings perched on old pilings have a certain charm. Graceful gulls circle overhead, and pampered sea lions bark and beg from the waters below. Most of the restaurants on this wharf serve sand dabs, squid and abalone, all local delicacies.

The new **Wharf Theatre** was built from the same plans as the former one which burned many years ago. Several well-known actors advanced their thespian careers in the old theatre, including Richard Boone. The rebuilt theatre has a proscenium stage with a balcony to permit Shakespearean plays and provide space for musicians.

If you want to try something really different, the **Sea Garden Diving Bell** is on this wharf. The huge steel cylinder has thick glass portholes and is completely air-conditioned. This observation sphere is lowered 30' below the water's surface for six minutes for viewing or photographing the underwater gardens and the many species of fish in Monterey Bay.

Municipal Wharf No. 2 is to the east beyond the parking lots. This pier was built in 1926 to accommodate larger ships coming into the harbor. It is the working wharf with wholesale fish warehouses at its end. You can watch commercial boats unload squid, tuna, sole, salmon, cod, kingfish, anchovies and herring and squawking gulls taunting fishermen as they clean their catches. Monterey is one of the leading squid ports in the United States, exporting hundreds of tons annually to Europe and the Philippines.

If you would like to do some drop-line fishing for tom cod or sunfish, bait is free with rod rentals on both wharves, and no license is required for saltwater fishing from a public pier. Arrangements for deep-sea fishing trips can be made on both wharves, too. You can launch your own boat from

Wharf No. 2. The **Monterey Peninsula Yacht Club** and its marina filled with bouncing craft are also here.

Monterey Municipal Beach, east of Wharf No. 2, is a sandy, mile-long stretch. A lifeguard is on duty during summer months in the area closest to the dock. The warm, shallow water in this spot is good wading for small children. The whole beach is good for sunbathing and picnicking. Open fires are not allowed, but you may use a camp stove or hibachi.

At the entrance to the tunnel leading to the Presidio is a typical small, double-ended fishing boat, the *Santa Maria*. Three generations fished from its decks. The monument notes the contribution of pioneer Sicilians to Monterey's fishing industry.

Follow the shoreline west to the **Presidio of Monterey** overlooking the harbor where dozens of fishing boats are moored. The Presidio was moved from its original level site near Lake El Estero in 1792 to these 409 hillside acres which command a dramatic view of Monterey Bay. While driving through the Presidio be sure to observe the strictly enforced traffic regulations; this is a military reservation. Most of the streets at the Presidio were named after distinguished members of the 11th Cavalry, stationed here during the early 1920s. However, Sgt. Beans, who had a road named after him, was a mongrel smuggled into the post to become the Cavalry's beloved mascot. The dog was even listed on the division's roster, and the entire 11th Cavalry stood at attention for Sgt. Beans' funeral.

Once reverberating with the sound of bugles, marching feet and horses' hooves, today the Presidio is the **Defense Language Institute**, the largest language school in the free world. Training is provided in thirty-five languages, including many dialects in each. The average daily enrollment is 3,200, representing all branches of the service. The 400-plus instructors are, with few exceptions, natives of the countries whose languages they teach.

One of the most historic spots on the Monterey Peninsula

is at the Pacific Street entrance to the Presidio. This 10′ monolith marks the approximate site of the **Junipero Oak** mentioned earlier. An ornate cross, the profile of Padre Serra and a bas-relief of San Carlos Cathedral are carved on the stone column. The boulder marker to the left commemorates Gaspar de Pórtola's official claiming and colonization of Alta California for Spain in 1770.

The large granite eagle sculpture on the hillside memorializes Commodore John Drake Sloat's landing at Monterey in 1846. He came to annex Mexican Alta California, which included what is now California, Nevada, Arizona, Utah and parts of New Mexico, Colorado and Wyoming, to the United States.

A tall wooden cross on the brow of the hill marks the site of a village of the Presidio's primordial inhabitants, the Rumsen Indians. Their settlement was an important one, judging from the large, pitted, nearly 2,000-year-old *rain stone* found in the area, a mark of distinction among Indian villages.

The Indian and military artifacts and photographs displayed in the **U.S. Army Museum**, below the eagle sculpture, trace the history of Presidio hill during Indian, Spanish, Mexican and American occupation. The museum is open from 11 A.M.–1 P.M. and 2–5 P.M. Wednesday, Thursday and Friday; from 10 A.M.–5 P.M. Saturday and Sunday; closed Mondays and Tuesdays.

Follow the shoreline once again to one of the most celebrated streets in the world—**Cannery Row**. Until Nobel- and Pulitzer-prize-winning author **John Steinbeck** drew world-wide attention to it, the street was called *Ocean View Avenue*. Steinbeck's novel *Cannery Row*, published in 1944, immortalized the oily setting and offbeat cast of characters who were actually a part of Monterey's booming sardine industry. This famed street also provided the setting for *Sweet Thursday*.

After whale and sea otter hunting diminished, Monterey again looked to the bay for resource. In the 1940s the city became *the Sardine Capital of the Western Hemisphere,* adding a new mystique to Monterey's reputation and a colony of

Cannery Row

Sicilian fishermen to its population. In a peak year over 200,000 tons of sardines were processed in plants on Cannery Row. The silver fish filled the city's coffers with gold until the mid-forties when they mysteriously disappeared from the bay. There are many theories about this phenomenon, some based on fact perhaps, others pure fancy. No one really knows why they left. Monterey's economy sagged and personal fortunes were lost as cannery owners auctioned their plants and equipment, and fishermen mortgaged their homes to keep their boats. A small fishing fleet still chugs out of the harbor in the early mornings and brings back catches to be sold on Fisherman's Wharf and to restaurants throughout the peninsula.

Old-timers who were not involved in the sardine industry are the first to tell you that they had no personal regrets about the sardines' departure. In Monterey's heyday when canneries worked round the clock, a malodor hung over the city for days at a time. Ladies held cologned handkerchiefs to their noses when going out. Cannery Row was certainly no tourist mecca in those days.

A hush fell over the Row as the canneries folded, and Monterey suffered another shock to its economy. Monterey recovered; the street was reincarnated with the new and the old standing side by side, and Cannery Row became one of the major attractions of the Monterey Peninsula.

Cannery Row starts at the Coast Guard pier. Monterey's base has two 95' cutters, *Cape Wash*, based at Monterey, and *Cape Hedge*, which is attached to Monterey but usually remains at Morro Bay to the south. Two smaller boats, 40' and 44', also work out of Monterey. The Coast Guard's primary mission in this area is "search and rescue."

The dock near the Coast Guard base is generally crowded with skindivers. They get in and out of their wet suits and inflate their brightly colored rafts next to their parked cars, which jam the vacant bayshore lots during daylight hours. Sea otters and sea lions entertain here, too, to the amusement of divers and a gallery of spectators.

In the middle of the nineteenth century, sea otters were hunted off the Central Coast for their desirable fur. This was an important economic factor to Monterey. The otter population in the Pacific once numbered two million, but by 1867 they had been hunted to near extinction. Fortunately, the sea otter has reappeared and has increased in numbers under government protection. Rafts of otters can be seen off Cannery

Row, along the Pacific Grove and Pebble Beach shorelines and at Point Lobos.

The most remarkable feature about the sea otter is that it is the only marine animal known to use a tool. Floating on his back, the otter places a large flat rock on his stomach, holds a shellfish, such as a mussel or turban snail, with both of his paws and then brings it down hard on the rock to crack it. Surely there is no more cunning sight in local waters than that of a mother sea otter floating leisurely on her back in a kelp bed and cuddling her baby on her chest, looking like a wet teddy bear, while both are rocked by gentle offshore waves.

Some dilapidated cannery buildings, with their salt-stained, cracked windows and weather-worn names on their sides, stand idle. This is the way the disappearance of the sardines left them. Many oil-soaked canneries have been destroyed by fire. Others have been renovated and now house an assortment of businesses. You will be in the midst of a new and different Cannery Row lined with restaurants and cocktail lounges, art galleries, specialty shops and antique stores. You'll never go hungry or thirsty on Cannery Row. Some of the Peninsula's finest restaurants are here, and it is also the center for much of the area's night life.

John Steinbeck wrote:

"Cannery Row in Monterey in California is a poem, a stink, a grating noise, a quality of light, a tone, a habit, a nostalgia, a dream. Cannery Row is the gathered and scattered, tin and iron and rust and splintered wood, chipped pavement and weedy lots and junk heaps, sardine canneries of corrugated iron, honky tonks, restaurants and whore houses, and little crowded groceries and flophouses."

His words are inscribed on the plaque of a bronze bust which stands under a cypress tree next to the sidewalk on the shoreside of Cannery Row near Prescott.

Cannery Row has not changed so much that you cannot imagine "Doc" Ed Ricketts (a real life character and Steinbeck's good friend) and his cronies reeling up the wooden stairs to his Pacific Biological Laboratory at 800 Cannery

Row, now a private club. Lee Chong's Heavenly Flower Grocery (Old General Store) across the street is as fascinating as it was in Steinbeck's day, but the "girls" are long gone from La Ida's Cafe (Kalisa's International Restaurant) next door. Surprisingly, current day Cannery Row characters are equally as colorful as Steinbeck's fictional ones. Some businesses have adopted names from Steinbeck's books to sustain the old Row atmosphere, but they are not actual sites.

Once eighteen canneries worked night and day, serviced by a fleet of 100 fishing boats. More than 4,000 names were on the membership rolls of the Cannery Workers' Union. Each plant had its particular whistle that blew to summon the workers. They streamed on foot down the hill from New Monterey or arrived by the cab-load. The last lone cannery closed in 1973. If the sardines return, no one will be ready to welcome them.

Three blocks up the hill from Cannery Row is a business and residential section called **New Monterey**, a name left over from other days. Actually it is one of the older parts of the city and sprang up during the sardine era. Fisherfolk and cannery workers lived on the hillside and some still do. Lighthouse Avenue is the main shopping district. Here you will find various businesses, including grocery stores, restaurants, antique shops, secondhand stores, a pottery workshop and **Scholze Park** at Lighthouse and Hoffman with a children's playground.

2.

Picturesque
Pacific Grove

■ San Francisco Methodists had been seeking a suitable spot for a seaside Christian resort for some time, and they found it on this northernmost point of the Monterey Peninsula. Indian tribes from the inland vacationed in these groves of pines and oaks many years before this, and restocked their larders with mussels, abalone, and fish.

In 1875 a group of ministers from the Methodist Episcopal Church formed the Pacific Grove Retreat Association and put an almost indelible mark on the customs and laws of the city. Their policies and restrictions concerning immorality extended one mile in all directions from the center of town. Pacific Improvement Company (forerunner of Del Monte Properties Company, now Pebble Beach Corporation) was formed, and land was purchased from Southern Pacific and from David Jacks, a wealthy rancher. A tent city was laid out on 30' by 60' lots. Furnished tents, heated by wood stoves, rented from $2.25 to $5.50 a week. At the close of each summer season, the striped tents were carefully packed and stored in **Chautauqua Hall**, 17th and Central Avenue, now used for many community events.

The stockholders of Pacific Improvement Company generously agreed that they would donate a site for a church and a parsonage to any religious organization that asked for property. Pacific Grove, as a Methodist retreat, held meetings outdoors or in tents. **St. Mary's-by-the-Sea Episcopal Church** was the first formal religious edifice to be built. Services have been held in this English Gothic building, at 12th and Central Avenue, since 1887. William H. Hamilton, a well-known Sacramento architect, patterned the original small chapel after one in Bath, England. It was 32' wide and 70' long with a 75' spire. In order to enlarge the little church and add a chancel, sanctuary and porch without marring its classic lines, it was sliced in two crosswise and three bays were added in the middle. The interior is finished in natural woods—walnut, pine, redwood and cedar. A pair of Tiffany glass lancet windows with white lilies and pink foxgloves are of particular interest. Soon local carpenters were copying St. Mary's Gothic styling as they built homes in the area. Other buildings have since been added to the Episcopal church property to accommodate the growing congregation.

Pacific Grove became a haven for other denominations, too. Catholics, Congregationalists, the Christian Church and Salvation Army all established churches here before the turn of the century. In the early 1900s the Christian Scientists, Baptists and First Assembly of God built their churches.

Southern Pacific excursions from the San Francisco Bay area brought hundreds of people to Pacific Grove; the round trip cost $1. During summer months three or four eighteen-car trains ran along the waterfront and spilled their passengers, so they could picnic on the beach, enjoy the seacoast or attend Chautauqua events. Picnicking on the Sabbath was ruled illegal in Pacific Grove; so the trains were discontinued on Sundays. By 1926 the Chautauqua era had ended.

The Methodists fenced their little compound, rang the curfew bell at 9 P.M. and locked the gates. There were rigid rules concerning dancing, drinking and public bathing. Bathing suits had to be made of "opaque material, which shall be worn in such a manner as to preclude form. All such bathing suits shall be provided with double crotches or with skirts of ample size to cover the buttocks." A far cry from today's bikinis! Whatever laws weren't on the books were understood anyway. While living in Monterey, **Robert Louis Stevenson** wrote about Pacific Grove: "Thither, in the warm season, crowds come to enjoy a life of teetotalism, religion and flirtation, which I am willing to think blameless and agreeable."

Expenses for running the campground were paid by selling lots for $50. each. Eave-to-eave, board-and-bat cottages sprang up on former tent sites and can be seen along the narrow streets between Lovers Point and Pine Avenue. Year-round residents built handsome mansions. Within ten years Pacific Grove became the *Cultural Center of the West*. The first Chautauqua (an assembly for educational purposes, combining lectures and entertainment) was held in a tent in June 1879 and later in the Old Chapel (Chautauqua Hall), designated a California Registered Landmark. The city hosted three Presidents: Benjamin Harrison, William McKinley and Theodore Roosevelt.

Pacific Grove was bounded by the beach on one side and by fences on the other three. The gate at the wagon and carriage entrance was kept padlocked. Peddlers and tradesmen from Monterey were forbidden to come in and sell their wares. In 1880 State Senator Benjamin Langford, who had a summer home nearby, grew tired of locking and unlocking the gate and took an ax to it. Thus Pacific Grove was dramatically freed from fenced-in isolation and joined the rest of the Monterey Peninsula. Fifty years later Dr. Julia Platt, a maiden-lady scientist and the city's first and only woman mayor, took an ax to another gate at Lovers of Jesus Point and earned her nickname "Lady Watchdog." The city later purchased this beach property, and it is now known simply as "Lovers Point." A Christian campground blossomed into a charming city and became incorporated in 1889. Pacific Grove's present population is 18,000.

Provincial Pacific Grove has relaxed at last. For ninety-six years the sale of alcohol was prohibited except for medicinal purposes; pharmacists were kept pretty busy filling prescriptions! In spite of the continuing efforts of the small Pacific Grove Retreat Association to keep the town dry, in 1969 voters broke loose from this restriction and today liquor is sold in what was then California's last dry town.

Pacific Grove is known as **Butterfly Town U.S.A.** and

rightly so. For over a hundred years tens of thousands of bright orange and black monarch butterflies (*Anosia plexipus*) have migrated each October from the Northern Pacific states, British Columbia and Southern Alaska to winter in the groves of trees, only to become restless and fly away to the north in March. This annual miracle is one of nature's mysteries and not yet scientifically explained. The Pacific Grove Museum of Natural History, Forest and Central Avenues, has an exhibit showing the monarch's migration pattern. The butterflies hang in huge clusters like dried leaves in the tall pines in **Butterfly Trees Park** on Lighthouse Avenue, at the Alder Street side of Washington Park and in scattered trees throughout the city. On sunny days what you might think is a dead tree will suddenly come alive in a burst of flaming color which slowly disseminates into lazy, velvet-winged butterflies fluttering over town gardens. Leave your butterfly net at home! The maximum penalty for molesting a monarch butterfly in Pacific Grove is a $500. fine and a six-month jail sentence! Hundreds of costumed school children herald the return of the monarchs every October by marching in the *Annual Butterfly Parade*, which is followed by the *Butterfly Bazaar*. Gordon Newell's granite sculpture of a monarch stands in Lovers Point Park, one of few monuments in the country honoring the insect world.

David Avenue is the dividing line between Monterey and Pacific Grove. Drive to the west end of Cannery Row, turn left, cross the tracks, turn right and you will be on Ocean View Boulevard and ready to peruse picturesque Pacific Grove.

Thousands and thousands of oval sardine cans were manufactured at the **American Can Company** (now filled with shops) on your left when Monterey was the *Sardine Capital of the Western Hemisphere.*

On the shoreside is **Monterey Boat Works**. Many of the fishing boats working out of Monterey during the sardine era were built here, and some are still in service. Now owned by Stanford University, the building has been renovated inside to provide enlarged facilities for **Hopkins Marine Station** on China Point, just ahead. The exterior has been restored to its original state. Hopkins Marine Station is an educational and research facility specializing in the study of intertidal life. It was the first marine laboratory on the Pacific Coast, established in 1891, and the third in the nation.

For more than fifty years a Chinese village thrived on **China Point** but went up in smoke quite mysteriously in 1903. Its settlers originally came to work in the Santa Lucia mines during gold rush days and drifted to the coast to resume a more familiar occupation, fishing. After the fire the Chinese established a community on Alvarado Street in Monterey.

Chinese junks followed the boat parade after the *Feast of Lanterns*, a tradition which began in 1880 at the close of each Chautauqua. This festival is held every year during the last week of July and is based on an Oriental legend about villagers searching with lighted boats and lanterns for the Mandarin's lovesick daughter, who was forbidden to marry her peasant sweetheart and ran off to drown herself. The Feast of Lanterns recounts the story with a week-long, city-wide celebration, including a lantern procession, a lighted boat parade, and the crowning of Queen Topaz, culminating with a huge fireworks display at Lovers Point, better than the Fourth of July.

Pacific Grove has a pleasing blend of old-fashioned and contemporary architecture with many beautiful homes typical of both eras. Several movies with New England settings have utilized Victorian homes here. The gazebo at the **La Porte Mansion** (formerly Pinehurst Manor), 1030 Lighthouse Avenue, was built by Warner Brothers in 1958 during the filming of *A Summer Place*, starring Troy Donahue and Sandra Dee.

Redwood plaques designate 182 homes built in Pacific Grove before 1890. A two-day *Victorian House Tour* is held each March so visitors can view interiors of some of these restored turn-of-the-century homes. A sampling of these proud mansions will be noted here as you travel along. It's easy to find your way around. If you get lost, just head toward the water and you will be back on your itinerary.

Pryor House, 429 Ocean View Boulevard, was built in

Green Gables, Pacific Grove

1908 for Mayor John P. Pryor. The foundation and surrounding wall are of massive hand-hewn stone. Third and fourth generations of the Pryor family still occupy this three-story shake manor.

When **Green Gables**, on the corner of Fifth Street, was built in 1888 by a Pasadena judge as a summer home, it was called Ivy Terrace Hall. Ivy cascaded from this Swiss Gothic down to the waterfront. It has been authentically restored as a guest house. Note that it faces three directions on three levels.

The gray castle-like home a few doors up from Ocean View Boulevard on Seventh Street is known as **Kinswood Tower** or **The Captain's House**. It was built in 1889 by Everett Pomeroy, who created a small replica of his family's castle *Berry Pomeroy* in Devonshire, England. The distinctive crenelated square towers resemble battlements.

The large house at 110 Tenth Street was built by the

Pacific Improvement Company in 1893 to be rented during the summer Chautauqua series. Originally it was closer to the water but was moved to higher ground in 1909.

Let the kids out to run at **Berwick Park**, the large grassy area on the shoreside between Hopkins Marine Station and Lovers Point, great for tossing frisbies or playing touch football or just loafing.

Lovers Point Park just ahead has picnic facilities, a volleyball court, children's pool and access to the sheltered beach. This is one of few safe wading and swimming beaches on the Monterey Peninsula. Be forewarned; the water's cold! In spite of the nippy average 55° temperature of the surface, hardy skindivers enjoy this spot, and surfers skim the huge waves when they break off the point. Rock fishing is good on the far side of the pier.

Once there was a large bathhouse, a Japanese tea garden, skating rink, bowling alley, even a windmill, at Lovers Point. All are gone. In the summertime, though, you can still take a ride in a swan-like, **glass-bottomed boat** and view the strange rock formations, unusual plant life, colorful fish of many species, shells of every hue and a forest of seaweed beneath the offshore waters. These glass-bottomed boats were first introduced in the area in the 1890s. The bottom of the boat serves as a three-dimensional screen, and a curtain is drawn when the boat reaches the viewing area. Each can carry sixteen adults and two children, and the trip takes half an hour. Scientists from all over the world have been attracted by the abundance of exotic submarine life in Pacific Grove waters. Jacques Yves Cousteau, the famed explorer and marine biologist, has visited the area several times.

Many national publications have featured Pacific Grove's **Magic Carpet of Mesembryanthemum**. A glorious mass of pink and lavender ice plant, interspersed with clumps of geraniums, marguerites, red hot pokers, veronicas, tea and yucca trees blooms from late April through August along the cliffs between Hopkins Marine Station and the Lighthouse Reservation. Winding paths and benches invite strollers. Hayes Perkins, a retiree, began planting the colorful ground cover across from his home in 1943 because it grows well in poor soil and requires very little maintenance. The city fathers took note of his successful experiment, and a crew was hired to complete the planting along the waterfront. Seeing the *Mesembryanthemum floribundum* in bloom at Perkins Park can make your whole visit to Pacific Grove worthwhile!

The three-mile shoreline is spectacular any time of the year, equally as beautiful as Seventeen-Mile Drive, and free to see. Pacific Grove is one of few California cities that owns its own shoreline. Because of continuing beach erosion and the disappearance of many small marine animals in recent years, collecting of all kinds is prohibited on these beaches. Park at the turn-out points. Feed the squirrels and chipmunks, but watch your fingers or you may need a tetanus shot. Look for sea otters playing in the kelp beds and the huge white grandpa seal lounging on his private rock and the interesting formation dubbed the "Kissing Rock." You can scramble down to the water, but be extremely cautious. The surf is unsafe; the undertow is quick and treacherous. If you feel like walking, there is a safe path between the street and beach from Lovers Point to the Lighthouse Reservation with welcome benches along the way.

The 18-hole **Pacific Grove Golf Links,** the only city-owned course on the Monterey Peninsula, is a fairly easy course and the least expensive of the public ones. Little **Crespi Pond** at its edge is a sanctuary for a variety of land and sea birds and is notable because it is a freshwater pond, yet very close to salt water. Also, look for the herd of deer roaming the golf greens.

If you have little ones along, you might turn left at Lighthouse Avenue, go a few blocks and drive through **El Carmelo Cemetery.** This isn't as mournful as it sounds. The entire Peninsula abounds with wild life, and you may see families of deer nibbling at the flowers in front of headstones.

It was the explorer Sebastian Vizcaíno who gave this headland the name "Point Piños" (Point of Pines). A sperm whale

Point Pinos Lighthouse

lamp first shone at **Point Pinos Light Station** in 1855 and was replaced in 1880 by a kerosene lamp. In 1915, the lamp was electrified; now a 1,000 watt bulb, magnified by lenses and prisms, produces a 50,000 candlepower beam visible for 15 nautical miles under favorable conditions. The light is 43' above ground and 89' above water. From one hour before sunset until one hour after sunrise and whenever daytime visibility gets below five miles, the light has a twenty-second duration flash with a ten-second eclipse. A standby generator automatically takes over during any power interruption. This is the oldest lighthouse in continuous operation on the West Coast and was a landmark for galleons taking the north circle route down the California coast to Mexico. The tower was damaged extensively in the disastrous 1906 earthquake and had to be rebuilt; however, the building, plus the old French Fresnel lenses and prisms, are the originals. The station houses a small museum of Coast Guard history and is the only lighthouse along California's 300-plus miles of coastline that is open to the public. You may visit any Saturday or Sunday from 1–4 P.M. Near the shore is the air diaphragm horn signal, which methodically comforts Pagrovians during foggy nights. Being on the road next to it when the foghorn blasts will give you a jolt, to say the least.

Lighthouse Reservation is a preserve for rare plants and a refuge for migratory birds and marine and land animals. The sandy setting has a foundation of granite, geologically eighty million years old; some was quarried for building the Light Station. Among the rare beach flora are lovely blue Tidestrom's lupine, one of the rarest, and butter-yellow Menzies wallflowers.

Beyond Point Pinos, the site of many preradar shipwrecks, you will be on the ocean side of Pacific Grove. A herd of seals, an otter or two and sometimes a sea lion inhabit the rocky cove of **Moss Beach.**

Adjoining the city is **Asilomar State Beach and Conference Grounds**, sixty acres of sand dunes and pine trees. Here hundreds of conventioneers gather annually. The Conference Grounds were originally founded by the Y.W.C.A. over sixty years ago, but now belong to the State of California and are run by Asilomar Operating Corporation, a nonprofit organization. Asilomar (pronounced *ah-seel-o-mar*) means "refuge or retreat by the sea." One of the finest conference centers in the country in a beautiful setting of forest and sea, Asilomar is unique in the State Park system.

The **California State Department of Parks and Recreation** has a **Training Center**, the first of its kind, at Asilomar. This facility provides formal classroom training for State rangers and park employees, with courses lasting one to five weeks. The average enrollment is twenty students. East Woods, the newest addition, also houses a research library for scholars.

Asilomar State Beach, between Point Pinos and Del Monte Forest, is a great place to stop. Hope you brought your old shoes! Poke around in the tidepools, run on the beach, play in the sand, watch the surfers if the surf's up, do some surf-fishing, eat your sandy sandwiches and generally enjoy a real ocean beach. Here, too, the surf is unsafe for swimming.

"Doc" Ricketts gathered specimens from the "Great Tidepool" mentioned in John Steinbeck's *Cannery Row* at Asilomar Beach. There are over 210 species of algae, more varieties than any other spot on the coast, because the northern and southern waters merge here. Please remember that California State law makes it illegal to collect any tidal invertebrates in State parks, recreation areas, State beaches and reserves. No general collecting is allowed between the mean high tide mark and a point 1,000' beyond the low tide mark offshore. Flowers, rocks, plants, animals and other natural features are protected by law. Driftwood may be collected from State beaches because it is not considered part of the natural environment.

You will be traveling east on Sunset Drive, **State Highway 68**. The **First United Methodist Church**, a quarter of a mile from Asilomar at the intersection of Sunset Drive and Seventeen-Mile Drive, was built in 1963 on a five-acre wooded site where deer nibble, squirrels scamper, birds sing, and frogs croak. The original Methodist Episcopal Church, which doubled as a town hall in the Retreat days, was in the downtown area and was torn down in the early sixties. While contemporary in appearance, the present church uses historic architectural forms and symbols. The mosaic-paneled front doors portray some of the major events of Christianity. The inspirational stained-glass "Resurrection Window" above the altar features parts of monarch butterfly wings. You are welcome to visit the sanctuary of Pacific Grove's founding church or attend Sunday services. If you are nearby just before noon any day, stop and listen to the person-played carillon as it fills the air with music.

Following **Highway 68** (**Holman Highway**) will lead you back to Highway 1, but you won't want to miss the rest of Pacific Grove; so turn left at Forest Avenue. You will pass two large retirement residences on either side, **Canterbury Woods**, operated by Episcopal Homes Federation, and **Forest Hill Manor**, operated by California-Nevada Methodist Homes,

Inc. Continue down the hill to Lighthouse Avenue. This is the middle of the downtown shopping area. There are no parking meters and, incidentally, no traffic lights downtown.

The green awning at 568 Lighthouse Avenue flags the entrance to **Pacific Grove Art Center.** Visitors are welcome to enjoy the galleries and studios where paintings, historical photographs, sculpture, graphics, and other creative arts are displayed in a Victorian setting. Hours are 11 A.M.–5 P.M., closed Sundays and Mondays.

Several of the city's finest old homes are along Lighthouse Avenue. **Gosby House Inn** was built in 1887 by a shoe store owner, J. E. Gosby, who also ran a boarding house for Methodist ministers. Later it was converted into a hotel with fourteen guest rooms and has remained that way for some seventy years.

Next door at 649 Lighthouse Avenue is **Hart Mansion** (now Maison Bergerac). Dr. Andrew J. Hart, a dentist, had the house built in 1892. The first floor was his office, and the family used the second and third floors as their home, just as the present owners do. Notice Dr. Hart's leaded sign over the front door and the beautiful stained-glass and stencilled windows. Gosby House Inn and Maison Bergerac are examples of Queen Anne architecture with their gabled roofs, angular bays, turret towers, and porches set inside the main structure frames.

Several elegant old homes in the business section have been rescued for use as professional offices; 721 Lighthouse Avenue is one. The Nova Scotian cobbler who built Gosby House Inn also built this attractive house in 1898. The turn-of-the-century interior provides a charming old-fashioned atmosphere for modern-day law offices.

In 1880 the Methodist bishop brought seed pods of eucalyptus trees from Australia, and they were planted in a double row along *Lighthouse Road.* Some of the largest blue gum eucalyptus trees can still be seen in front of the post office at Lighthouse and Congress Avenues.

If you go back and walk toward the water on Forest Ave-

Maison Bergerac

nue, you will come to the **Pacific Grove Chamber of Commerce**, just a block below Lighthouse. The office is open 9 A.M.–5 P.M. Monday through Saturday. The staff will be happy to answer your questions and provide free brochures. An up-to-date street map of the entire Monterey Peninsula is inexpensive, and you will find good use for it later at Pebble Beach and in Carmel.

Along the way is one of the first houses built in Pacific Grove, 164 Forest Avenue. Many small cottages and some larger homes were built over original tent platforms. When this two-story, no-nonsense frame house was constructed around

1884, the canvas tent was left inside the walls as insulation. The boxy style and stick-work porch are typical of cottages built at that time.

The name of the double-turreted old hotel at 612 Central Avenue was a combination of the Spanish word *estrella* (star) and *Central*. **Centrella House** served as headquarters for Methodist ministers and their families when they came to participate in the retreats. It is one of the city's oldest hotels, built in 1888.

Only 177 museums throughout the United States and Canada have been accredited by the American Association of Museums; the **Pacific Grove Museum of Natural History** is one of thirteen in California to receive such accreditation. As long ago as 1935, the Association called this museum "the best of its size in the United States." It features monarch butterflies, marine and bird life, shells, and Indian artifacts and has a native plant garden outdoors. A relief map of Monterey Bay shows the great submarine canyon on its floor, 8,400' down, a gash deeper than the Grand Canyon. This tremendous chasm is one of the reasons why Monterey Bay has always been a fishing port. Upwelling waters bring nutrients to feed surface organisms which in turn provide food for the bay's fish. Museum hours are 10 A.M.–5 P.M., closed Mondays. Admission is free. The *Annual Wild Flower Show* is held here in April and the *Water Color Show* in September.

Pacific Grove Public Library, also on Central Avenue, was the first to be established in Monterey County in 1880. Their collection of over 1,250 volumes pertaining to the South Seas is the most comprehensive of its kind in the West and contains many rare works, including those by explorers Hakluyt, Vancouver and Cook, ancient maps and atlases, even handwritten logs from clipper ships and windjammers.

For relaxing, **Jewell Park** is across the way; this is where the enormous brown tent used to be raised for prayer meetings. Another good sit-down spot is the Solarium atop Holman's Department Store on Lighthouse Avenue where you can enjoy a panoramic view of Monterey Bay. Holman's, which has served the Peninsula since 1891, was mentioned in *Cannery Row*. For a number of years **John Steinbeck** lived in a cottage in Pacific Grove, built by his father around 1900. Much of his research for *Cannery Row, Sweet Thursday* and *Tortilla Flat* was done here.

There are fine municipally owned tennis courts up the hill behind the **Community Center**, 515 Junipero Avenue. Children can exhaust themselves at the playground here before climbing back into the car. More tennis courts are located at the high school on Sunset Drive, available when school is not in session.

Washington Park (twenty acres) on Sinex Avenue, near Seventeen-Mile Drive, has complete picnic facilities including barbecue pits. There are lots of trees, many with butterflies in them during the season.

Most of the motels are in the area around Asilomar Avenue and at the west end of Lighthouse Avenue, plus two at Lovers Point.

Christmastime is special in Pacific Grove. A Winter Parade welcomes the season. The Assembly of God's Yuletide gift to the community is a wonderful singing Christmas tree at the corner of Pine and Fountain Avenues with nightly performances the week before the holiday. The First Church of God presents a nativity pageant nightly. There are two outstanding areas where whole neighborhoods participate in outdoor decorating. One is Egan Avenue, just a few blocks up from Ocean View Boulevard; the other is "Candy Cane Lane" in Country Club Heights, a residential section just east of Forest Avenue. It is impossible to miss finding either place because they are so brightly lighted, and you can follow the parade of cars filled with wide-eyed children. You'll see poinsettias the size of small trees in bloom in many Peninsula gardens this time of year, too.

Now that you have a whole roll of film of Pacific Grove, "the change-of-pace place" on the Monterey Peninsula, reload your camera. It's time to see Pebble Beach and the world-renowned Seventeen-Mile Drive.

3.
World-Famous
Seventeen-Mile Drive, Pebble Beach

■ Pebble Beach, where stately mansions hide in verdant woodlands and emerald fairways meet sapphire sea, is not a vast private residential park by accident. This greenbelt and majestic beach front, totaling 8,400 acres, were acquired in the early 1900s by their present owners, Pebble Beach Corporation (formerly Del Monte Properties Company), under the presidency of the late Samuel F. B. Morse, grandnephew of the developer of the Morse Code. The Corporation has strict building codes governing the preservation of the area's beauty and bounty of nature. Guidelines for the 6,000-plus residents and for visitors have been established for the protection of native flora and fauna. Rules prohibit disturbing plant or animal life of any kind.

Under Sam Morse's leadership, buildings erected within Pebble Beach's boundaries were to be "Spanish-Colonial or Monterey style of architecture." Cypress Point Club, designed by George Washington Smith, is a perfect example of the Monterey style Morse had in mind. With the passage of years, rules about building have been relaxed. Now there are homes and mansions varying in style all the way from Colonial to Mediterranean to futuristic.

The original **Seventeen-Mile Drive**, planned fifty years ago, began and ended at the Old Del Monte Hotel in Monterey, now the Naval Postgraduate School, and encircled the entire Monterey Peninsula. It was more like a thirty-five-mile drive.

Now it is routed only through the confines of Pebble Beach Corporation's land.

The exclusive atmosphere of the area is obvious right away. There are toll gates at each of the four entrances to this impressive community. Country Club Gate and Lighthouse Gate are in Pacific Grove; Carmel Hill Gate is midway up the hill from Monterey off Highway 1; and the one in Carmel is just plain Carmel Gate off North San Antonio Avenue. Residents have special license tags and come and go freely. Others must pay the $4. entrance fee (well worth it) to see the world-acclaimed Seventeen-Mile Drive. This gate fee is refundable if you plan to dine or stay at The Lodge at Pebble Beach (formerly Del Monte Lodge). If you have friends who live inside the gates, phone and ask them to call the security guard at the gate you intend to enter and you will be admitted free of charge. There is a well-marked bicycle route along the Drive; bikers are required to get permits at the gate. Traffic laws are strictly enforced.

You will be provided with a map of Seventeen-Mile Drive showing points of interest along the yellow-and-orange painted line when you pay the gate fee, but do not stray too far from this designated route unless you have a complete map showing all roads, or you are sure to get lost and spend several hours trying to find your way out. The natives are friendly, though; so ask a pedestrian or knock on a door and the butler will gladly direct you.

From Lighthouse Gate in Pacific Grove, below the First United Methodist Church at Sunset Drive and Seventeen-Mile Drive, the road follows the low, white sand dunes and winds through exclusive residential sections past showplace homes of some of America's most prominent citizens. You'll recognize their names on the gateposts. The coastline changes from sandy dunes to jagged crags where ships have met their doom. Gnarled, wind-blown Monterey cypress trees, which grow indigenously nowhere else in the world, offer unusual subject matter for camera buffs. Huge offshore rocks are populated by resting birds and relaxed seals; deer gaze unconcernedly on lawns and golf greens. In the spring mother seals teach their babies to swim in the sheltered coves. A sudden geyser of water ejected from the ocean, then a visible dark hump, denotes the presence of a passing whale in the spring or winter. Shaded picnic areas, miles of winding bridle trails, coves of quiet beauty, and stretches of sandy shore enhance Pebble Beach. Many sights are described on the back of your map, but there are still some interesting sidelights along the way.

Camera Obscura (Latin for *dark room*) is near the picnic area opposite Seal and Bird Rocks. The little round building, designed by John Carl Warnecke, has only one door and no windows. There is a circular screen in the floor, and while the lens rotates showing close-up views of **Bird Rock, Seal Rock, Fanshell Beach** and parts of two golf courses, a recorded commentary tells their stories. There is no charge for using this walk-in camera.

The thirty-eight-acre campus of **Robert Louis Stevenson School** is off Forest Lake Road. This private college preparatory, independent secondary school was founded in 1952 for boys in grades nine through twelve, but now girls are also registered.

The much-photographed **Lone Cypress** is the most famous of its species, Monterey cypress (*Cupressus macrocarpa*). Its survival against the elements has been aided by guy wires. Undaunted in its struggle, this rarest of trees has managed to perpetuate itself by producing a young cypress growing out of its roots. Unsuccessful attempts have been made at transplanting Monterey cypress trees, but they will thrive only in this restricted habitat at the bleak headlands on either side of Carmel Bay. This is the only place in the world where you can see stands of these remnants of the Pleistocene Age. In protected **Crocker Grove**, the indigenous cypress retain their normal straight and tall characteristics, but washed by sea spray and lashed by winds, they cling tenaciously to the rocky shoreline of Cypress Point and become misshapen and grotesque.

According to Fanny Osbourne Stevenson's memoirs, Rob-

Witch Tree, Pebble Beach

ert **Louis Stevenson** drew on his vivid memories of walks along the Drive for descriptions in his immortal classic *Treasure Island*. He described these twisted trees as "ghosts fleeing before the wind." Each of the holes at **Spyglass Hill Golf Course** is named after one of Stevenson's fictional characters, such as, "Long John Silver," "Blind Pew" and "Jim Hawkins."

Pescadero means *a place where fishing is done*. **Pescadero Point** forms the northern arm of Carmel Bay. On foggy nights the diaphanous figure of "the Lady in Lace" has been seen wandering near the bleached-bone-white **Ghost** and **Witch Trees**. It is assumed that she is the restless spirit of Maria del Carmen Garcia Barreto Madariaga who once owned and twice sold Rancho El Pescadero which extended from Seal Rock to Carmel.

Thirty-four miles of riding trails wander through Pebble Beach's glorious tree-and-sea setting. Twenty-seven acres of woods and grassy fields along Portola Road are the grounds of **Pebble Beach Equestrian Center**. In the early 1920s the stables here were used by Del Monte Hotel guests. Through the years horsemanship has become a happy pastime for many Peninsulans. The Equestrian Center sponsors a full season of events: shows, meets, races and the "game of Kings," polo. **Collins Polo Field** is across the way and is where teams from all over the country gather for the *National Rugby Championship* every March.

Dominating the dramatically laid out golf courses along the natural shoreline is **The Lodge at Pebble Beach** with its fancy restaurants and exclusive shops. Elite groups rule the Pebble Beach social scene: **Cypress Point Club, Beach and Tennis Club** and **Stillwater Yacht Club. Monterey Peninsula Country Club** is on its own lovely knoll in Del Monte Forest.

The Lodge at Pebble Beach is one of the world's great resorts and has played host to a passing parade of celebrities. The John F. Kennedys vacationed here before he became President. Golfing Presidents have always taken time out to swing their clubs at Pebble Beach. Surrealist painter Salvador Dali spent a series of summers at The Lodge. The antics of Dali, Oliver Hardy and W. C. Fields who sauntered onto the golf course, drink in hand, cigar in mouth and umbrella overhead, still provide table talk during dinner parties. Clark Gable was one of The Lodge's regular guests, getting in a little golf between pictures.

Golf can be enjoyed 365 days a year on five championship courses: **Pebble Beach, Cypress Point, Monterey Peninsula Country Club's shore and dunes courses** and **Spyglass Hill.** Pebble Beach, Spyglass and **Peter Hay Par 3** are open to the public. Major tournaments, like the annual televised **Bing Crosby Pro-Am,** are played on three challenging courses within the gates. Pebble Beach Golf Links were chosen as the site of the 1972 U.S. Open.

The late Jack Neville, a member of the winning U.S. Walker Cup team at St. Andrews, Scotland in the 1923 tournament, designed **Pebble Beach Golf Links** along with Douglas Grant. Neville, although not a golf architect, laid out the course over half a century ago, and it is still considered

Spyglass Hill Golf Course

famous, or infamous, for its great climax, the 18th hole. Speaking of the 18th, Neville said: "The worst thing you can do is hook because it's ocean all down the left side."

George Washington Smith, designer of Cypress Point Clubhouse, also planned the **Crocker Marble Palace**, the car-stopper as you approach Pebble Beach through the Carmel Gate. It is the first waterfront mansion you see, recognizable by its many arches. Also called **Byzantine Castle**, this ornate baroque mansion is one of the most notable along Seventeen-Mile Drive and was built and decorated between 1926 and 1931 for Mrs. Templeton Crocker of the railroad and banking family. Later she married Paul Fagan, a California and Hawaii entrepreneur, and for awhile the house was called the "Crocker-Fagan Mansion." The interior is mostly of Italian marble with mosaic floors, marble baths, archways, and loggias. There are forty-five different arches in the garden, using thirty-two different types of marble. Another extravagant feature is the beach heated by underground pipes. It is said that leftover marble was unceremoniously dumped into the water below when the house was completed.

Some of the stately homes along the Drive have hand-carved signs at their portals indicating how their owners' fortunes were made. *Wit's End* still identifies the home of the late cartoonist, Jimmy Hatlo. There is a spool of thread on the signpost at the entrance to the Coats' residence, of Coats and Clark fame.

In recent years celebrities from the world of entertainment have settled at Pebble Beach. Clint Eastwood, like his parents, has lived here for many years, long before he became an international star. Joan Fontaine and Doug McClure, more recent residents, are also active in the social life of the Peninsula. Seeking privacy, Gene Hackman is among a number of notable newcomers who have established Pebble Beach residences. Doris Day, Merv Griffin, William Windom and the White brothers of *Earth, Wind and Fire* have homes in Carmel Valley, while Kim Novak and Paul Anka have chosen Monterey's Jack's Peak area. Only their realtors and good friends know for sure exactly where all of them live.

Many Pebble Beach estates, now too costly for private ownership, have been sold or leased to large corporations and

Pebble Beach Golf Links

are maintained year-round as guest quarters for V.I.P.'s or vacation retreats for executives.

As much as you have read or heard about this scenic wonderland, now that you have seen it, you will agree that Seventeen-Mile Drive rivals the Riviera and has managed to exceed your expectations.

4.

Cozy
Carmel-by-the-Sea

■ Indefinable Carmel-by-the-Sea is a captivating village that is really "by-the-sea." The city traces its heritage back to 1602 when Sebastian Vizcaíno, after claiming Monterey for Spain, camped for a month near Carmel River before sailing away to report his new discoveries to the King of Spain. Vizcaíno named the sea and the land after the Carmelite monks who accompanied him on his voyage. Carmel was first settled in 1771 when Padre Junipero Serra moved the Mission from Monterey to the more agreeable and arable setting of Carmel. Most of the neophytes were Costanoan Indians.

The village proper, less than a square mile in size, didn't really burgeon until the early 1900s when it attracted a colony of artists, authors, and musicians. Their nonconformist way of life still prevails in Carmel. The 1906 earthquake left many of San Francisco's bohemians homeless. Poet George Sterling and novelist Mary Austin urged them to follow their lead to Carmel. Their small homes nestled in the forests and edged the sandy beaches. Mary's tiny "winter wickiup" with a treehouse workroom in a close-by pine was near the Mission. A group of citified professors built vacation cottages; one was David Starr Jordan who later became the first president of Stanford University. One of the blocks of Camino Real is still referred to as "Professors' Row."

Among the distinguished writers associated with Carmel's early days were Jack London, Sinclair Lewis, Jimmy Hopper,

Upton Sinclair, William Rose Benét, and Robinson Jeffers. For awhile it was the home, too, of the talented and prolific Belgian mystery writer, Georges Simenon, who created the famous character "Maigret," a French criminologist. Also, there is a house on San Antonio Avenue that is still called "Lincoln Steffens House" even though it has changed hands many times. Steffens was a feared, muckraking journalist who developed an absolute phobia for noise in his later years and retired to Carmel before his death in 1936.

Well-known artists who appreciated the soul-searching solitude and stimulating beauty of Carmel were Jules Tavernier, Arthur Hill Gilbert, and Percy Gray. Stanton Delaplane, newspaper columnist and former Carmel resident, wrote about the town in those days: "Most of Carmel's storekeepers were artists. While packaging eggs, they gave little lectures on the effects you could get with gouache."

This diversified group set a pattern for preserving their surroundings that is still rigidly observed. One of the township's first acts was to draw up an ordinance to protect the trees. Rather than felling a tree when the winding streets were laid out, the planners simply split the road to curve on both sides of the cherished tree. This puzzles yet delights visitors whose hometowns may be concrete jungles. Showing utter disdain for progress, Carmel's latter-day pioneers decreed that there would be no street lights nor sidewalks in residential districts. Nowhere would there be high-rise buildings or neon signs, and commercial ventures would not sully the wide white beaches. Even AAA signs and public telephone booths are custom-made to suit Carmel's rules. This means that Carmel is notable for other facilities that it does not have: no traffic lights, no parking meters, no courthouse, no jail, no cemetery, and no mortuary.

The log of laws passed by Carmel's governing boards over the years, often with humor and always with thoroughness, has kept casual charm under control. Take Ordinance 60 passed in 1925 under a section entitled "Obnoxious Industries Zone No. IV." "Obnoxious industries" included were "stables, soap factories, match factories, chemical works, sawmills, and other industries of similar character."

A few years ago city fathers approved an ordinance prohibiting outdoor displays of "plastic plant materials or other simulated plant materials." It has to be the real thing—no imitations for Carmel!

Mayor Perry Newberry, a former San Francisco journalist, was one of the leading crusaders for preserving the city's unique independence. To keep progress from spoiling Carmel, he suggested installing toll gates at its entrances! He felt that home mail deliveries were unnecessary, and to this day many villagers go daily to the friendly staffed post office at 5th and Dolores to pick up their mail and exchange pleasantries with their fellow citizens. Reading the bulletin board outside the post office will give you an insight into their way of life.

Because of city officials like Newberry, there are no honky-tonk strips of motels, gas stations, or hot dog stands. In 1929 a zoning law ruled that business development should be forever subordinate to the residential character of the community. Carmel-by-the-Sea, with a present population of 5,000, remains a charming collection of flower-bowered cottages and regal residences in the heart of a pine forest bordering Carmel Bay.

From Highway 1 there are two entrances to Carmel, Carpenter Street and Ocean Avenue. Taking the Carpenter Street entry, at the first signal light if you are driving south, will take you through a residential area, a proper introduction to this one-of-a-kind village. When you reach the "Y" a short way down the hill, take Serra Avenue until you come to "the statue." Once it was suggested to the city council that this weathered oak sculpture by Jo Mora be moved to a more suitable location where it wouldn't be threatened by errant drivers. Residents protested loudly that Carmel-bound visitors would lose their way if they didn't have Padre Junipero Serra to guide them, so here he stays.

Jo Mora was commissioned by Samuel F. B. Morse, who established Pebble Beach, to carve this statue in 1922. Mora,

Father Junipero Serra

a native of Montevideo, Uruguay, studied art in New York and Boston and moved to the Monterey Peninsula in 1920 when he was assigned to design and execute the much-admired sarcophagus of Padre Serra at Carmel Mission. Mora died in 1947 and in that year was one of only eight persons whose names had been included in *Who's Who in America* since the book's inception.

"Turn left at the statue," as Carmelites have been directing visitors for over half a century, and follow Junipero Avenue to the business district.

Houses in the village proper have no numbers, so their distinctive architecture is a great help in finding a friend's home for the first time. Architectural emphasis has always been on individual expression. Even service stations are pleasing to the eye, some in Spanish style, others with modern Oriental overtones. One thing is certain: there is no such thing as typical Carmel architecture. There are redwood board-and-bat homes, adobe dwellings, sturdy log cabins, Spanish villas with high-beamed ceilings and stone-flagged floors, ultramodern mansions designed by world-famous architects, and then there are the Hansel-and-Gretel houses designed by Hugh Comstock. The latter have given Carmel its most lasting sobriquet: *A Storybook Hamlet.* The Tuck Box, a tearoom at Dolores and 7th Avenue, has this touch of Grimm and is an outstanding example of Comstock's "dollhouse period."

Hugh Comstock built a large doll-like house for his wife, Mayotta, so she could display and sell her handmade "Otsy Totsy" rag dolls. Friends found the little fairy-tale shop so "adorable" that Comstock was commissioned to build full-scale houses similar to it. These storybook-illustration homes are easily spotted along Carmel's winding, wooded streets. Comstock later perfected waterproof adobe bricks and built houses of these, with redwood shakes and hewn timbers adding character.

Other architects responded to natural settings, designing seashore homes with a Mediterranean influence. English cot-

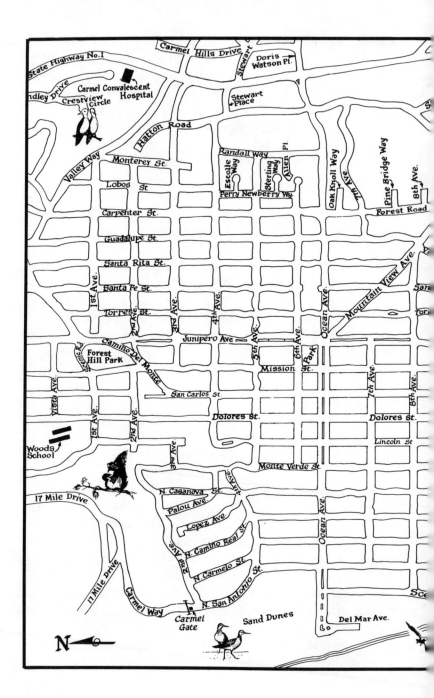

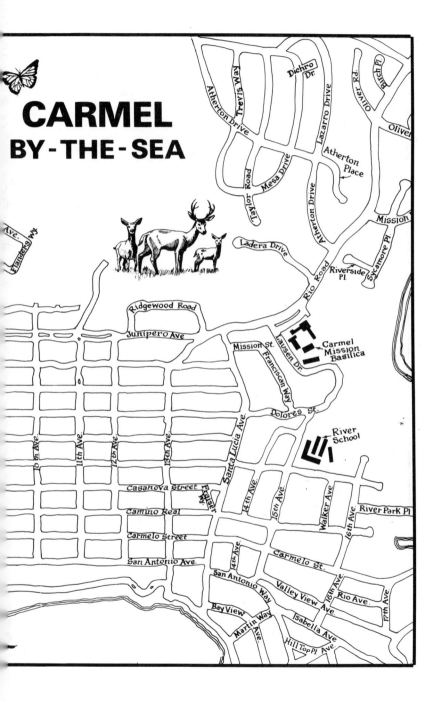

CARMEL
BY-THE-SEA

tages, one with an imported thatched roof (across from Carmel Mission) and New England salt boxes stand side by side.

Plan to spend a whole day in Carmel; if you don't, you will wish you had! Instead of having to run back to your car and move it every hour or two to avoid a ticket, park several blocks north or south of Ocean Avenue, the main business street, where there are no limiting signs. Remember where you left your car; it is not uncommon for Montereyans and Pagrovians to lose track of theirs in Carmel. Carmel is for walking and gawking, filled with hidden courts which could never be discovered while driving. You might do well to follow Carmel's "L.O.L.'s" and wear tennis or low-heeled shoes as some sidewalks are not paved and have dips and protruding tree roots.

Carmel Business Association is the village's chamber of commerce. Their offices are upstairs in Vandervort Court on the west side of San Carlos between Ocean Avenue and 7th. Ask for free copies of *Guide to Carmel-by-the-Sea*, which includes a good map showing all the hideaway courts, and *The Gallery Tour of Carmel-by-the-Sea*. Carmel has always been a popular place for weddings and honeymoons; *How to Get Married in Carmel* gives all the details if you're planning a wedding here. The Association's offices are open 9:30 A.M.– 4:30 P.M. Monday through Friday, closed Saturdays and Sundays.

Carmel's champagne-in-a-teacup atmosphere charms both young and old and provides a welcome escape from the hasty pace of big cities. There is something about the scintillating sunshine, contrasting tender mists, and downright fogs that makes even the retired put aside the idle life. Carmel-by-the Sea is a community of everyday-and-Sunday painters, poets, potters, and putterers. In Carmel society you may find the attractive matron who checked your groceries in a gourmet market during the day sitting across from you at an elite dinner party in the evening.

Civilized, friendly Carmel-by-the-Sea is a city of serendipity. You have to do the exploring and discovering yourself.

Window-shop along the main streets, of course, but meander back into arcades and courts, too. Be sure to look up or you will "underlook" some of the most interesting shops. Don't be reluctant about browsing; shopkeepers love "lookers" and you will not be high-pressured into buying.

The world's wares are in these shops, a potpourri of many things, pretty and practical. From way-out boutiques to staid salons, you'll find an extensive collection of clothing to fit any taste and any budget. Kitchen and bath shops and interior design studios offer the latest in home fashions. Enticing scents identify the many candle shops. Delicately detailed European Christmas ornaments, authentic Indian, Eskimo and African artifacts, imaginative toys, high-flying kites, all-period antiques, exotic shells, fascinating weather instruments, intricate needlework, prohibitively priced gems, and affordable handcrafted jewelry—the list goes on and on.

It will be hard to pass by bakery windows filled with flaky-fresh pigs ears, alligator bread and gooey-good pastries, and candy stores with homemade, hand-dipped chocolates, and hand-pulled taffy. There are markets with smelly imported cheeses and hanging salamis and all manner of irresistible food and drink.

From a great hamburger in a gruff atmosphere to the finest French cuisine in an elegant brocaded setting, there is a place to dine to suit every taste and every pocketbook. Unless you relish engrossing conversation or maybe a game of darts, chess, or checkers in a cozy bar, night life is nonexistent in Carmel. City law prohibits live entertainment, even juke boxes, in hotels, restaurants, and cocktail lounges.

There are few independently owned hotels left, and Carmel has two of them. Guests used to arrive at the **Pine Inn** on Ocean Avenue by stage. This is Carmel's oldest inn and has been a part of the village scene for three generations. A Victorian atmosphere is created by old prints, marble-topped tables, velvet-flocked wallpaper, and memorabilia of yesteryear.

La Playa Hotel at Camino Real and 8th, four blocks from

the village, has been a part of Carmel's tradition since the early part of the century when it was a huge private estate. Old-world decor is pointed up by conversation-piece furnishings throughout, and an Hispanic flavor is added by festive Mexican artwork.

Rest at **Devendorf Plaza**, the park off Ocean Avenue which was named for one of the town's first developers, J. Frank Devendorf. He and another entrepreneur, Frank H. Powers, acquired most of the acreage now known as Carmel in 1902. They leased and sold lots, preferably to people with artistic inclinations, for "a few dollars down and pay the balance when you can." Devendorf and Powers were interested in the arts and supported institutions like the Arts and Craft Club, formed in 1905, and **Forest Theater**, one of the first open-air theaters in the country "whose pillars are primeval pine and whose roof is the sky." A concave hillside gives every seat a perfect view of the stage. Forest Theater was constructed in 1910 and has been presenting Shakespearean productions and concerts ever since.

Numerous fine art galleries show and sell the works of local artists and artisans and those of other artists from all over the world. You can watch weavers, potters and sculptors at work in their own studios. There are close to one hundred galleries and studios, each as absorbing as the next. Hotels, motels and galleries all have free walking guides to simplify finding these artistic spots. If you think you're not the gallery-browsing type, give it a try, anyway. You might be surprised and become so enthusiastic that you'll want to return tomorrow and finish your gallery-hopping. A small painting or sculpture will tuck in a suitcase and would be a worthwhile remembrance of your visit to the Monterey Peninsula.

As the number of artists increased in the 1920s, it became evident that they needed a showcase. In 1927 a group of painters formed the **Carmel Art Association**, and then came the depression. Meetings and exhibitions were held in members' galleries. Finally in 1934, the Association purchased an old studio at Dolores and 6th Avenue and renovated it. This gallery is open 10 A.M.–5 P.M. daily.

A private art school, **Carmel Art Institute**, Monte Verde and Ocean Avenue, was founded in 1938 by Armin Hansen and Kit Whitman. Guest lecturers and teachers, such as Fernand Leger, Alexander Archipenko, and Frederic Taubes, have appeared here. The school was purchased later by Pat and John Cunningham, both artists. Mr. Cunningham was involved in one of Carmel's most mysterious happenings. In the early 1940s he invited San Francisco sculptor, the late Beniamino Bufano, to attend the opening of the Bach Festival. When Bufano's large stainless steel statue of Bach, especially executed for the occasion, was due to be unveiled, it was discovered that the 800 lb. bust had been spirited away. To this day it has never been found.

The **Cherry Foundation** at Guadalupe and 4th is a combination art gallery, schoolroom and performing arts center. The gallery is open 2–4:30 P.M. Wednesday through Sunday. Carl Cherry invented the Cherry rivet gun, which makes blind riveting without explosives possible and proved invaluable during World War II ship– and plane–building. The Cherry rivet made the Foundation possible, a lifetime dream of Cherry and his artist wife, Jeanne D'Orge.

The village's annual attractions range from kite-flying and sand castle building to the glorious two-week long **Annual Bach Festival** held in July at **Sunset Center**, San Carlos and 9th. This Festival, now in its fourth decade, is the largest and most popular live music event within easy reach of Pacific Coast residents and enjoys the patronage of many out-of-staters. Sunset Center's theater, with its excellent acoustics, good parking, and proximity to lodging and dining facilities, is the perfect setting for this auspicious event.

The cultural complex at Sunset Center has an assembly hall which seats 750 and various other meeting rooms which accommodate 40 to 250 people. The studios offer short-term instruction in various art forms for visitors. The galleries and studios are open to the public.

Bach Festival performance

The **Church of the Wayfarer**, on the corner of Lincoln and 7th Avenue has a Biblical garden, a pleasant place to pause and gather knowledge at the same time. Plants, shrubs, and trees are all labeled with their common and generic names and with chapter-and-verse references to the Bible.

Sometime during the day, you are bound to say: "But where's the beach?" It's at the foot of Ocean Avenue, and on a clear day you can see the ocean from the top of the hill. Walk a few blocks straight down the hill and you'll be there. **Carmel Bay** is between **Cypress Point** and **Pinnacle Point**. The beach is wide, white, and sandy. Sunbathing and picnicking are favored pastimes; swimming isn't safe.

From early morning until late at night on the Fourth of July, Carmel's beach is crowded with picnickers. Sometimes a whole neighborhood or an entire club membership comes en masse. A day that grows foggy has never kept Carmel's citizenry from celebrating their independence. The beach front glows with campfires as night falls and roman candles

send streaks of color to the sky. If you're spending Fourth of July weekend in Carmel, don't be bashful about joining the festivities.

The **Great Sand Castle Contest** was an event begun in 1962 just for family fun, free of written rules. The exact date is never announced until a few days before, but is usually held in early fall. Categorical prizes and Sour Grapes Awards are given by judges who are local architects. Entries range from the profile of an ex-President to a full-sized Volkswagen. Sometimes there are no castles at all for the tide to wash away.

You won't want to miss **Scenic Road** along the tree-bordered bay or Carmel Mission Basilica. Drive toward the beach on Ocean Avenue and turn left on Scenic Road. Go slowly along this narrow, twisting, one-way street and enjoy the views on both sides—enviable homes and enticing beaches.

Poet **Robinson Jeffers' Tor House** and adjoining **Hawk Tower**, constructed entirely of granite found along the shore,

Robinson Jeffers' home—Hawk Tower at Tor House

are the most striking of the many architectural styles in Carmel. The stone house was patterned after an English Tudor barn Jeffers had seen and admired. The 40', three-story tower, built as a musical retreat for his organist wife, Una, is an adaptation of an old Irish tower. Two portholes salvaged from a local shipwreck were installed in the walls. Jeffers, a semirecluse, came to Carmel in 1914 to devote full time to writing. Much of his poetry bears a direct relationship to the natural landscapes of this coastline. People come from all over the world to see this fabled stone house, many from Czechoslovakia where Jeffers developed an almost cultlike following. Jeffers' son Donan and his wife Lee have initiated efforts to preserve Tor House with the National Trust for

Historic Preservation. **Harrison Memorial Library** at Ocean and Lincoln has an extensive, valuable collection of selected works by Robinson Jeffers.

Local tour guides are no different from their breed elsewhere and like to season their lectures about important sites with a little spice about scandals. They point out the love nest on Scenic Road called **Benedict Cottage**, where famed evangelist Aimee Semple McPherson spent ten days with her then-current amour, Kenneth G. Ormiston, a former radio operator at her Temple. Believing her concocted impression that she had been kidnapped from her ornate Angelus Temple in Los Angeles, police from all over California searched for Aimee until her tryst in Carmel came to light. She was later indicted by the Grand Jury on a false kidnapping charge.

Walker House on **Carmel Point** was designed by **Frank Lloyd Wright**. Jutting out on a rocky arm and surrounded by water on two sides, like all of Wright's masterpieces, it appears to be an intrinsic part of the natural surroundings.

On **Twelfth Night** (twelve days after Christmas) Carmelites bring their dismantled Christmas trees to the foot of 13th Avenue. A gigantic fire blazes on the beach while hundreds of onlookers participate in the traditional ceremony marking the close of the Christmas season and the beginning of Epiphany. The light of the fire heralds the start of a new year; the tides swallow the remnants of the old.

Another typical-of-Carmel activity, first held in 1930, is the **Annual Kite Festival** at Carmel High School on Highway 1, held in windy March. All kites competing in ten categories must be handcrafted. The Festival attracts hundreds of participants and spectators.

Scenic Road rounds the point and becomes Carmelo Street. Turn right on 15th Avenue which will lead to the **Basilica of Mission San Carlos Borromeo del Rio Carmelo.**

Originally built in 1771, this Mission was Padre Junipero Serra's headquarters until his death in 1784 and his favorite of the nine he personally founded. He is buried at the foot of the altar. The first adobe church was replaced by a larger

Basilica of Mission San Carlos Borromeo del Rio Carmel

stone edifice in 1797 under the direction of Padre Fermin de Lasuen. In 1834 the Mexican Government, then ruling California, ordered the secularization of the Missions. The Franciscan Fathers were sent back to Spain, and Carmel Mission, without their guidance, was abandoned in 1836. The Indians, who tended the corrals, vast grazing lands for sheep and cattle, and farming acreage, were left homeless and helpless and became scattered throughout the territory. Typical of these was "Old Gabriel," whose grave is in the small cemetery in the Mission courtyard. At the time of his death, he was considered "the oldest man in the civilized world." More than three thousand Indians are also buried in the cemetery beside the church.

The first steps toward restoration of Carmel Mission took place under Father Ramon Mestres in 1924. Sir Harry Downie, renowned authority on California Mission architecture and present curator, along with Father Michael D. O'Connell, took over and completed the task. Since 1933 the Mission has been the parish church.

The stateliness of the Mission's early days interwoven with the Peninsula's past is obvious the moment you push open the bare wooden door leading to a courtyard reminiscent of Spanish–Colonial times. The impressive stone church with its tower dome is surrounded by well-kept gardens. There are two museums on the grounds which are supported by voluntary contributions. They are open 9:30 A.M.–5 P.M. weekdays and 10-30 A.M.–5 P.M. Sundays. The array of practical and religious treasures reveals the hardy, industrious, and austere lifestyle of Padre Serra and the Franciscan monks who were his contemporaries. The kitchen and tiny modest room where Serra slept have been reproduced.

Ignoring the electronic marvels of modern science, the art of campanology has been revived at Carmel Mission. Seven workable bells, some dating back to the early 1800s, are rung by pulling ropes, the same way it was done over two hundred years ago.

In 1960 Pope John XXIII elevated Mission San Carlos Borromeo del Rio Carmelo to the highly dignified rank of Basilica, one of only eleven churches so designated in the United States and one of only two Basilicas in the western states.

5.

Pastoral
Carmel Valley

■ In the late 1800s Robert Louis Stevenson described Carmel Valley in *The Old Pacific Capital* as "a true Californian valley, bare, dotted with chaparral, overlooked by quaint unfinished hills. The Carmel runs by many pleasant farms, a clear and shallow river, loved by wading kine." Novelist **Mary Austin** chose this region as a setting for *Ysidro*, a story of Mission days in quiet Carmel Valley, and **John Steinbeck's** paisanos hunted frogs in the river's marshes.

Many Indian artifacts have been found on Carmel Valley ranches. Long ago tribes moved up and down the valley, to and from the coast according to the seasons. Early settlers acquired their acreage through Spanish and Mexican land grants. As early as the 1830s, the pasture lands were divided into enormous privately held grants: Rancho Cañada de la Segunda, Rancho Potrero de San Carlos, Rancho San Francisquito, Rancho Los Laureles and Rancho Tularcitos.

The 64,000 acres of this unincorporated drowsy valley, stretching fourteen miles east of Carmel, are surrounded by the steep beginnings of the rugged Santa Lucia Mountains to the south and the high ridge of the Peninsula to the north. The 14,000 residents live in homes varying from the unpretentious to the pretentious; some sprawl graciously along the Carmel River banks while others hang by their chimneys on the cliffsides.

Carmel Valley's climate is warmer than elsewhere on the

Peninsula, so the landscape is punctuated with resorts, restaurants, theaters, equestrian, tennis and golf facilities—some public, others posh and private. The hotels and motels are more than just places to stay overnight; all offer a variety of interesting activities. There are large orchards and truck gardens, dude and cattle ranches. Roadside stands have fresh fruits and vegetables grown in the valley, and along Carmel Valley Road are a Christmas tree farm, begonia gardens, a succulent farm, and a chicken ranch where you can buy newly laid eggs.

Carmel River flows thirty miles northwest through the coastal ranges to south of Carmel. Steelhead season opens in mid-November and runs through February. Whether or not fishing is good depends on rainfall and the amount of water released by Los Padres and San Clemente Dams upstream. If you are over sixteen, you will need a license for freshwater fishing.

Deer and mountain lion hunts and special wild boar hunting expeditions are conducted in the Santa Lucia Mountains. Russian wild boars were brought to this country from the Ukrainian Mountains in 1919 to a hunting preserve on the border of North Carolina and Tennessee. Thirteen boars were shipped to Monterey County in 1924. They mated with runaway domesticated swine, and hundreds now roam the far regions of the Santa Lucia Mountains. Boar hunting is not for beginners; the average boar weighs 250 pounds, a dangerous and fast prey.

The entrance to the valley is a few miles south of Carmel to the east of Highway 1. Neighboring shopping centers at the mouth of the valley, Carmel Rancho Center, The Barnyard, and Carmel Center, are connected by a road at the rear. Picnic fixings can be purchased at the supermarkets or delicatessens here.

Rancho Cañada Golf Club (public), a mile east, has two side-by-side courses winding back and forth over five bridges across Carmel River, clubhouse facilities, pro shop, bar, and dining room.

Carmel Valley Village

You will go by the entrances to two adult communities, **Hacienda Carmel** and **Del Mesa Carmel**, and a retirement community, **Carmel Valley Manor**, operated by Northern California Congregational Retirement Homes, Inc., before you reach mid-valley.

On the north side of the road, opposite Via Mallorca, is **El Encino del Descanso** (*The Oak of Repose*). Indian carriers stopped to rest under this time-bent oak while transporting their dead to burial.

The award-winning architecture of **Quail Lodge**, adjoining **Carmel Valley Golf and Country Club** (private), is worth seeing. The notices posted on the sides of the buildings at neighboring Valley Hills Shopping Center will give you an insight into the rural feeling of the area.

Turning right at Schulte Road will lead first to **Riverside Park** and then to **Saddle Mountain Recreation Park** beyond, both with recreational vehicle facilities, campsites and picnic facilities. This locale was first an Indian campground because of the adjacent river and later a Mexican land grant to Loretta Onesmina de Peralta in 1837. Saddle Mountain, a mile in from Carmel Valley Road, has a 3½-mile hiking trail leading to an elevation of 1,000' for a superb view of Moss Landing, the Santa Cruz Mountains and Los Padres National Forest.

Berwick Barn on Berwick Drive is a Carmel Valley landmark and has captured the imagination of local artists and photographers for many years. Changing its face and color with the seasons and even with the time of day, the barn never appears the same in any two paintings. Englishman Edward Berwick raised this picturesque building in 1869 as the first improvement on his 120-acre ranch, where he cultivated Winter Nelis pears which became world-famous and were shipped to many European markets. In the early spring fragrant white blossoms can be appreciated here and there on the few remaining pear trees which were once a part of huge orchards. **Berwick Manor and Orchard** has been nominated for inclusion in the National Register of Historic Places. Much of the original Berwick homestead, which was purchased for $500. in gold, has been sold off. A granddaughter lives in the first home on the remaining twenty-nine acres. The house, part of which dates back to the 1840s, still has hand-hewn beams tied with rawhide. The Berwicks entertained **Robert Louis Stevenson** several times, but he was always banished to the barn to sleep because the hostess was suspicious of his eczema-scarred hands and consumptive cough.

The photogenic **old sand plant** at Robinson Canyon Road has been in operation for half a century. Natural sand and gravel, extracted from the Carmel River bed, is the exclusive product of Valley Rock and Sand Company. For ecological reasons, dredging can be done only when the river is running, so the operation is spasmodic.

Carmel Valley Riding and Polo Center on Robinson Canyon Road offers professionally guided trail rides for the entire family. Guides will escort riders high into the mountains and meadows along the river banks. Small-group rides are geared to individual levels of proficiency. Excursions leave the stable at 10 A.M. and 1 P.M. Tuesday through Saturday.

The Korean Buddhist Temple, Sambosa (Three Treasures), just off Robinson Canyon Road, is situated on 7½ secluded acres facing the gently flowing river with serene mountains as a backdrop, a setting similar to that of its sister temple in Seoul, Korea. The unusual shade of lavender on the Temple's facade is characteristic of the Korean sect of Buddhism. The natural wood structure is Oriental in theme and spirit, gracefully blending East and West. Serious students come here for 100-day retreats involving intensive meditation. The public is invited to attend regular Sunday services at 11 A.M.

Robinson Canyon Road continues south through redwood groves and a cool, wooded canyon. About ten miles down the road, on the site of a former Angora goat ranch in the Santa Lucia Mountains, are the weathered relics of some wooden buildings. **Robert Louis Stevenson** lived in one of these tumbledown cabins for a short time during the fall of 1879. Suffering from "galloping consumption," which eventually caused his death, the author left Monterey to escape the penetrating fog and save on lodging expenses. After being thrown from his horse, Stevenson anguished under a sheltering tree for two nights before Anson Smith, a bear hunter, and Jonathan Wright, the goat rancher, found him. The two mountain men nursed Stevenson back to health. While recup-

Robert Louis Stevenson's cabin

erating, the famed author was moved to write this requiem: "Beneath the wide and starry sky, dig a grave and let me lie . . ."

A rustic sign 8½ miles out Carmel Valley Road, just before Los Laureles Grade intersection, marks the entrance to **Garland Ranch Regional Park** (541 acres), Carmel Valley's first park and the initial acquisition of the Monterey Peninsula Regional Park District. The gates are open from 8:30 A.M. to sunset. No motorized vehicles are allowed in the park, so stop your car in the designated area, then cross the footbridge. Trail maps and a bird identification pamphlet are available at the visitors' center, the frame building just across the river. Drinking water and restrooms are here. Miles of clearly marked nature trails offer hikers a choice of easy, short walks or an arduous climb to 800'-high **Inspiration Point** for a panoramic view of the mountains and valley. Equestrian trails lead through oak-studded hills and broad mesas to mountain tops. There are picnic areas but no formal lawns, play equipment nor barbecue pits. The beauty of this park is its total emphasis on nature at its best—wildflowers and wildlife in their natural habitat, hidden glades, expansive meadows, a waterfall, and a lot of sunshine and fresh air. In all, this scenic parkland is a place to picnic, hike, ride, fish for steelhead in season, or just see and enjoy.

Los Laureles Grade goes north and connects Carmel Valley Road with State Highway 68, the Monterey-Salinas Highway, at a point about midway between Monterey and Salinas. The road is about six miles over the mountain tops and has been designated a Scenic Highway, indicated by the California poppy symbols on road signs.

Continuing east on Carmel Valley Road, you will come to the **Boronda Adobe.** Don José Manuel and Maria Juana Boronda built their home on the west side of Boronda Road, near its intersection with Carmel Valley Road, and in 1840 became the first in-residence ranchers on huge Rancho Los Laureles. The once crumbling adobe was altered and added to through the years and has been lovingly restored for use as a private residence. The old part is of interest architecturally. It is 64' long and 19' wide, and the thick walls have been well-preserved.

When her husband was crippled in a horseback-bullfighting accident, Doña Boronda turned to cheese making to support their fifteen children. Using an old family recipe, she produced "Queso del Pais" (*cheese of the country*) and began marketing it. Her venture was so successful that other dairy ranchers in the valley began making cheese, too, in order to use up excess milk. The White Oak Properties complex on Carmel Valley Road, between Paso Hondo and Esquiline Road in the heart of the village, housed the Boronda's dairy business. The white clapboard building with the odd cupola was a cooling

Boronda Adobe

house for milk and cheese. David Jacks, a canny Scotsman and leading Monterey businessman, discovered Maria's cheese. He already owned several dairies that he leased on a share arrangement, so he started these farmers in the cheese making business. Jacks' Monterey Cheese soon became known as "Monterey Jack Cheese." However, old-timers attribute the name to the heavy house jacks which were used to fasten the tops of the kegs in which curds were mashed in order to squeeze out the whey. Northern California is still the only place where Monterey Jack Cheese is manufactured.

Hidden Valley Music Seminars, an Institute of the Arts at Ford Road, was organized to bring young artists, students, and teachers together in the most productive environment possible. Five-week seminars are held during the summer to train young people for the professional world of music. The dormitory behind the theater will accommodate eighty students. Musicals are presented at Hidden Valley and at Sunset

Center in Carmel. Their Children's Theater Division brings live professional productions into classrooms throughout the Monterey Peninsula.

The **Madonna of the Village**, between Hidden Valley and the post office complex, spreads joy, peace and love. The village is the business and social center of the valley. There are many craft and gift shops and art galleries to explore and a number of excellent restaurants in or near the village. **Robles Del Rio Airport**, about a quarter of a mile northeast on El Cammito Road, is a normally fog-free, 1,800' airstrip suitable for single and light twin-engine planes.

On a hot summer's day, a dip in the **Old Swimming Hole** is a good way to cool off. Take Equiline Road, off Carmel Valley Road just beyond the library. The cliffs at Porter's Cove, north of Equiline Bridge, form a natural diving board for the swimming hole.

Beyond the village, Carmel Valley Road becomes Tularcitos Road. Turning south on Cachaugua (pronounced *ka-shaw-wa*) Road for about ten miles will take you to **Prince's Camp**. In the 1920s this was an informal hunting and fishing campground with a small store and saloon. Today it is a little community of mobile homes clustered around a busy bar and a busier store.

Just beyond the turnoff to Prince's Camp is the entrance to **COMSAT (Communications Satellite) Earth Station**. A thirty-four-ton parabolic dish antenna, standing taller than a ten-story building, is focused on a communications satellite 22,300 miles away. This is part of a network involving eighty countries, so that important news events can be televised simultaneously around the world. Visitors may take guided tours between 1 and 3 P.M. Wednesdays. It would be wise to call ahead to let them know you are planning to come (659-2293). If the staff is short-handed, sometimes tours have to be cancelled. A brief movie concerning the operation of the Station is shown; then a technician explains the complicated electronic equipment, how the signal is received and transmitted to the satellite. The Earth Station is not classified; you may take pictures. Leave your pets in the car and keep track of your children. No picnicking is permitted on the property.

A few miles farther is **Los Padres Reservation**. Park your car near the Ranger Station and walk to the reservoir, owned by California-American Water Company, about half a mile on a dirt road. There is a U.S. Forest Service Park here. Trout fishing is good in season; power boats are not allowed on the lake, just self-propelled. This park is crowded in summertime and on sunny weekends. Hiking is a back-to-nature experience, and this is one of the starting points to the profusion of trails throughout Los Padres National Forest. You must sign in at the Ranger Station if you intend to hike into the wilderness.

Cachagua Road joins Tassajara Road. **Jamesburg**, a small unincorporated settlement at the junction, was named after its founder, John James from North Carolina, in 1867. A monument on the site of the first post office honors the James Family. The first settlers filed three kinds of claims: homestead, preëmption, and timber, each 160 acres. This meant that individual family members could pool their 480-acre claims to make a fair-sized cattle ranch. Early cabins were built on sled runners so they could easily be moved from claim to claim. The settlers lived off the land for the most part. Winters were hard and when ready cash was needed, they trapped live grizzly bears and hauled them off to Monterey in oxcarts to be sold for bull-and-bear fights. They also gathered ladybugs by the handful in the caves at Chews Ridge and sold them to Salinas Valley farmers for use in their fields—the forerunner of modern pesticides. At the turn of the century when Tassajara Hot Springs, to the south, was a popular health spa, stagecoaches carrying vacationers left Salinas at 6 A.M. and arrived at Tassajara at 6:30 P.M., a distance of fifty-three miles, stopping at James Ranch along the way.

Hastings Natural History Reservation, on the north side of the Jamesburg–Arroyo Seco Road, encompasses two thousand unspoiled acres along Finch Creek. Once a working cattle ranch, the Reservation is now owned by the University of California and is managed by Berkeley's Museum of Vertebrate Zoology. Botanists and zoologists from around the world come to Hastings to study plant and animal life in a real environment away from laboratory conditions. Students and researchers stay from a few weeks to a few years. Since 1937 the forest and grazing lands have been left untouched to allow them to return to their natural state. You will understand why the Reservation is not open to the public and picnicking, hunting and domesticated animals are forbidden on the property. Visitors are usually ecology, college or nature groups who come for tours and lectures.

From Jamesburg the road winds another six miles to **Chews Ridge**, the destination of many outdoor enthusiasts who come in the summertime to enjoy camping and hiking and in the wintertime to try out their seldom-used sleds on the snow-covered slopes. From the ridge there is an eagle's-eye view of Los Padres National Forest, north to Salinas and west to Big Sur country and the Pacific Ocean. The caves near Chews Ridge were often used as shelter by the extinct Esselen Indians, a small tribe of only a few hundred. Writings on cave walls indicate that they were later inhabited by Costanoans who hunted wild game in the area.

The Santa Lucia Mountains provide some of the finest spots on earth for stargazing. The first independent astronomical observatory established since World War I, **Monterey Institute for Research in Astronomy**, is atop Chews Ridge on a site leased from the U.S. Forest Service. The small observation and research facility is just big enough to house a telescope, necessary computer equipment, and two or three astronomers at a time; consequently, it is not open to the public. If you brought along your own telescope, though, this is a tremendous spot to use it because there are no artificial lights to compete with the heavens.

China Camp, south of Chews Ridge, has a Ranger Station and full facilities for overnight camping. Beyond here the road becomes more difficult.

Tassajara Hot Springs, at the end of the road, deep in an isolated valley amid the lofty Santa Lucia peaks, were known to the Indians and later to the Spaniards for their chalybeate qualities. The name "Tassajara" comes from the Spanish-American word *tasajera*, meaning *a place where meat is cut in strips and hung in the sun to dry*, in other words, jerky.

From 1904 on, Tassajara became a fashionable retreat with a large brownstone hotel, which burned in 1949, and rustic buildings and bathhouses along Arroyo Seco Creek. For a distance of 200 yards, 17 hot mineral springs issue from the mountainside at a temperature of 140–150° F. The water contains sulphur, sodium, magnesia, iron and phosphate.

The road into this forty-eight-acre property was built in the 1880s by Chinese laborers. While the road is much improved, it is still an hour-and-a-half drive from Carmel Valley village. It is winding, scenic, and somewhat precipitous, definitely a low-gear journey.

In 1967 the Zen Center of San Francisco purchased Tassajara Hot Springs Resort, and it is now headquarters for Zen study and training in North America. New buildings have been added, and the mineral baths have been developed in the Japanese tradition. In the summertime visitors are welcome during daylight hours. For a reasonable fee you can picnic and enjoy the baths. Overnight reservations must be made well in advance. The dining room is open to overnight guests only; emphasis is on simple vegetarian food. Tassajara is closed to the public during winter months when the Center is used only for student training.

6.

Breathtaking
Big Sur Country

■ Big Sur is the name given to the ruggedly beautiful seacoast country stretching south from Carmel River to the southern Monterey County line. This now famous coast route is one of the world's most spectacular highways and an inspiration to poets, painters, and photographers. Seventy-two scenic miles connect the Monterey Peninsula with Southern California. Prior to the opening of Highway 1, it took half a day over a narrow, unsafe road through dense thicket and virgin timber to travel from Monterey to Big Sur. Before that there was only a horse trail for hauling supplies to the few inhabitants along the coast.

Highway 1 was built at a cost of ten million dollars, took sixteen years to build and was opened in 1937. During its construction, men lost their lives and equipment plunged into the sea. The road was plotted to take advantage of the breathtaking views as it hugs the natural rocky-coved shoreline, twists along steep cliffs, spans canyons formed by rushing rivers, and ambles along foam-fringed ocean beaches. At some places the road ascends almost 1,000' above sea level, then sweeps grandly around a point and descends to within 50' of a comely cove. The dramatic contrast between the restless, sometimes vehement sea and the serene beauty of primitive forests and magnificent mountains is unforgettable. Big Sur is an oasis in a day when wilderness is fast disappearing.

More species of birds are found in this coastal area than

anywhere else in California. Many animals, from mice to mountain lions, thrive in its forests. The phantom white orchid grows high in mysterious canyons, while rare ferns and wildflowers lace the inland streams.

The first residents of Big Sur country were the Costanoans or *coast people*, who hunted sea lions but lived mainly on a diet of fish and shellfish, supplemented with nuts, berries, and roots, seasoned with seaweed.

In Spanish "Sur" means *south*. Big Sur country took its name from Rancho El Sur, where early settler John B. R. Cooper and his family lived when they were not in Monterey. Cooper took the name "Juan Bautista Cooper" when he adopted Mexican citizenship. A shrewd trader, he accumulated much wealth and land, including Rancho El Sur.

The best time to drive Highway 1 is between noon and 6 P.M. when the inspiring views are not shrouded in coastal fog. Be alert at the wheel; this road changes with the turns, the hours, the days, and the seasons. Make sure you have film in your camera, take your time and marvel at the drama of each unfolding scene of this unduplicated seacoast called Big Sur. It's full of big surprises!

For over half a century globe artichokes have been cultivated along both sides of Highway 1 on the flat plain near the mouth of Carmel River. The State purchased the western 155 acres next to the road which eventually will become a natural park. The view of the ocean from the highway will be preserved, and there will be no sophisticated developments, such as playgrounds and overnight campgrounds. Open space will be cherished and the environment protected, another milestone in saving our precious land.

The **Little Red Schoolhouse**, in its enviable acre-and-a-half setting of trees, sand dunes and beach south of the artichoke fields, was built in 1879 and had an uninterrupted flow of children through its doors for nearly a century. At first it was a one-room schoolhouse serving children from the Carmel area. In 1952 Bay School became a parent cooperative nursery school under the auspices of Carmel Unified School District. During the past several years the school's future was dubitable. The termite-ridden little historical building had to be demolished when costs for restoration to meet today's standards proved prohibitive. Concerned citizens rallied, and an exact replica has been constructed on the same site.

The highway drops to sea level at **Monastery Beach**, a part of **Carmel River State Beach** (106 acres), which is crowded during good weather with swimmers, surfers, skindivers, sunbathers, and surf-fishermen. The lagoon at the mouth of the river is better for small children. There are no facilities of any kind at the beach or lagoon. When the river is running, it is possible to paddle your canoe or kayak into the lagoon's marshes for birdwatching.

On the hillside is the **Monastery of Our Lady and St. Theresa**. From their rooms the nuns can gaze out across the mind-calming sea or contemplate the tree-covered hills behind their imposing home. They lead a strict, cloistered life, stressing poverty, seclusion, silence and work, with prayer taking priority. Their lifestyle is little different from that of St. Teresa de Avila who renewed the then 400-year-old Order of Discalced (barefoot) Carmelites in 1562. A nunnery was established in a frame building on Carmel Point in 1925; the Monastery was opened six years later. The sisters raise vegetables in their gardens, and their food supply is supplemented by many donations of fruit, eggs, cheese, and fish. They do not eat meat. Four beehives produce honey. For income the nuns stitch vestments, do sacristy laundry, and make gift items which are sold at the Monastery and the Hermitage Shop in Carmel. The chapel is open to the public from 8 A.M.– 5 P.M. every day. The sisters who greet you have not taken the optional vow of silence. People of all faiths are invited to attend Masses or Sunday benediction or just visit and renew their spiritual strength.

The nuns you may see enjoying the beach across the way are Sisters of Notre Dame, a teaching order. The smaller building near the Monastery is **Villa Angelica**, their summer home.

San Jose Creek is several hundred yards south of the

Monastery. Gaspar de Portolá and his men passed through this area in 1769, still trying to identify Carmel River and Monterey Bay on the basis of Vizcaíno's descriptions. Padre Juan Crespi offered mass in a nearby meadow where, on a previous expedition, Portolá had erected a cross and buried a letter beneath it lamenting his failure to find Monterey Bay.

Just south of the semicircular cove at San Jose Creek Bridge, where Japanese fishermen once harvested abalone, is the entrance to **Point Lobos State Reserve**. Artist Francis McComas described Point Lobos as "the greatest meeting of land and water in the world." It is said that **Robert Louis Stevenson** used Point Lobos as a model for Spyglass Hill in *Treasure Island*, the classic adventure tale he wrote for his stepson, Lloyd Osbourne, whom he loved very much. Words are still inadequate; Point Lobos must be experienced.

To get the most from your visit to Point Lobos State Reserve, wear low-heeled shoes and comfortable clothing, take along a coat or sweater, and don't forget your camera. Plan to spend several hours enjoying concentrated natural beauty. The park is open from 9 A.M.–7 P.M. daily. A map will be provided at the gate when you pay an entrance fee. Hikers and bicyclists are admitted without charge unless they are planning a picnic. Very few roads mar this primitive area; most of it can be seen only on foot over unobtrusive trails. You can drive through the entire Reserve to trailheads and to the picnic area. There is no overnight camping. Swimming is permitted at **China Cove**, and boats can be launched at **Whaler's Cove**. Remain on the marked trails and enjoy all of Point Lobos for its beauty is unequalled.

State rangers conduct guided tours twice daily in the summer and on a lesser schedule off-season. Visitors are taken to six areas: Cypress Grove, Pine Wood, Bird Island, North Shore Trail, Whaler's Cove, or the sea lion area. In the summertime when weather and tides permit, there are early morning guided tidepool walks.

Point Lobos derives its name from its colonies of California and Steller's sea lions. You can hear their hoarse barking emanating from **Punta de los Lobos Marinos** (*Point of the Seawolves*). The California sea lion is the most intelligent of all of its kind and the one usually used in trained seal acts. The Steller is larger and least controllable.

Before white men came, Indians had overnight campsites at the Point while they fished and gathered abalone and mussels along the shoreline. Point Lobos has had a string of owners since. During the Mexican regime, this natural wonderland changed hands in a card game and became the unofficial property of a group of Presidio soldiers. At various times it has been the site of a smugglers' cove, whaling station, abalone-drying yard and cannery, and a cattle ranch.

In the 1860s Portuguese whalers operated a station at Carmelo Cove (now Whaler's Cove). This was a foul-smelling business with huge hunks of whale meat on the dock, cauldrons of boiling blubber emitting dense black smoke, shouting men, and screaming gulls. The oil was shipped out to be used in lamps and machinery. In the 1890s Japanese fishermen had an abalone cannery at Whaler's Cove.

Once Point Lobos had an unsuccessful coal mine. Gold and mineral mining ventures also failed. Rocks from a quarry here were used to build the United States Mint at San Francisco and Monterey's old jail behind Colton Hall. Much later, following the attack on Pearl Harbor in 1941, the Army's Signal Corps was stationed here for nine months.

Land speculators had been eyeing Point Lobos with avarice for many years. In 1933, with the help of the Save-the-Redwoods League, Point Lobos passed into the trusteeship of the State of California from the heirs of A. M. Allen, a man who appreciated the natural qualities of this well-preserved, almost primeval area. It is truly the crown jewel of the California State Park system. In 1968, the National Park Service designated this 1,250-acre Reserve a Registered National Landmark.

There are over 300 species of plants and 250 species of vertebrates and invertebrate animals and birds in this outdoor museum. The **Monterey Cypress**, known in the Pleistocene

Monterey Cypress

era, is making its last stand in the Monterey Peninsula region. Only a half-mile strip is left in the world. There are two small areas where this famous tree still grows naturally, one at Pebble Beach and the other at Point Lobos. In the spring acres of wildflowers brighten the landscape. Sea otters are always frolicking offshore. **Bird Island** is a sanctuary for thousands of land and sea birds. Point Lobos is also the northernmost breeding ground of the California brown pelican. The conglomerate pebbles here, ranging in size from your thumbnail to several inches, are the only record known of rocks from the Eocene Period.

Point Lobos has the first undersea **Ecological Reserve** in the nation, 750 acres of submerged land. With permission, underwater studies are carried on by individuals, universities, and private research groups. Skindivers must obtain permits (for looking and picture-taking only) at the Park entrance.

Point Lobos has been a favorite on-the-spot site of moviemakers for many years. In the 1920s and 30s, scenes from *Foolish Wives, Evangeline* and *Paddy, the Next Best Thing* were filmed here. The most recent was *Jonathan Livingston Seagull*. Since then stricter regulations are in force to avoid endangering the land and life of Point Lobos.

It will be difficult to leave Point Lobos behind, but there is much more of beautiful Big Sur country to see. Spindrift Road, down the way, winds toward the ocean past a long-established residential area, **Carmel Highlands**, where costly homes cling to rocky ledges and hang over the crashing surf. One of the area's most distinguished residents is **Ansel Adams**, famed nature photographer, who has produced major exhibits throughout the country and authored more than thirty books.

Joseph Victorine sighted this point from a whaling vessel in the early 1870s and made up his mind to settle here. He returned to the East Coast, packed up his family and moved out West. The Victorines settled on the site of the present Bay School but later built a home on this promontory where they established one of the first dairies in the area in 1899. Victorine sold out to a land development company in 1928, but it failed during the depression. Another Yankee, Charles G. Sawyer, purchased the property in 1948, and Victorine Creek was renamed "Yankee Point." Sawyer subdivided and elegant homes began cropping up on the precipitous cliffs.

The research program at **Behavioral Sciences Institute** at Carmel Highlands deals with human behavior of all kinds. The Institute also offers year-round reading and language therapy for all ages and trains school teachers to train others in fluency and articulation. Their Children's House deals with language and behavior problems of preschoolers, and they also have a Hearing Aid Center in Monterey.

Yankee Point has a superb view of the craggy coastline and is an especially good spot for whale-watching. In November you can watch California gray whales migrating to their breeding and calving areas in Lower California and see them return in the spring to their feeding grounds in the Bering Sea, an eleven thousand-mile journey. These huge mammals are 30–50' long and weigh about a ton a foot.

Little **Malpaso Creek** doesn't seem too forbidding now, but early accounts tell of difficulties pioneers had crossing it. In fact, an angry settler named it "Malpaso" (*bad crossing*). Carmelo Land and Coal Company operated a mine in the canyon here until the early 1900s. The coal was hauled to Point Lobos to be shipped out.

From **Soberanes Point** south to Point Sur is a **California Sea Otter Game Refuge**. Sea otters were hunted for their valuable furs until they were nearly extinct. Now protected, their population has increased. You can see them cavorting about in the tangled kelp along the coast.

The path at **Granite Canyon Bridge** goes down to the sea where there is a small waterfall with natural arches and grottoes. **The California State Fish and Game Mariculture Laboratory** at Granite Canyon is a center for the study of mass cultivation techniques for seafood items, such as red abalone, Pacific oysters, and Carmel Bay prawns. This research benefits both commercial and sport fishermen. The public is invited to visit the Laboratory during a one-day annual open house held in May.

Garrapata (*wood tick*) Creek wanders through **Garrapata Canyon** to the ocean. This is a residential area with many rustic homes along the lushly bordered stream.

Palo Colorado means *tall redwood* in Spanish. A paved road leads into this narrow canyon lined with redwoods and healthy ferns with cabins along the creek. It goes to **Bottchers Gap**, the beginning of many hiking trails into Ventana Wilderness, and beyond to **Pico Blanco Boy Scout Camp**. At the helicopter landing, there is a striking view of Little Sur Valley, Double Cones and Pico Blanco in the Santa Lucia range.

Ventana Wilderness is in the heartlands of the Santa Lucias, a part of Los Padres National Forest. This area is accessible only by trails. Hikers and campers need Wilderness Permits from the U.S. Forest Service before starting out.

Notley's Landing, across from the entrance to Palo Colorado Canyon, was an early-day lumber boomtown and busy seaport. Split redwood posts and pickets were loaded on boats by ship-to-shore cables. Tanbark was also exported, as well as lime from a kiln in the canyon. Old Notley's Landing was the prototype for the setting of *Zandy's Bride*, starring

Bixby Bridge

Liv Ullmann and Gene Hackman, but filming was done farther south at Molera Ranch. The story was based on a novel entitled *The Stranger* by the late **Lillian Bos Ross** who lived on Partington Ridge with her husband, **Harrydick Ross**, sculptor and woodcarver.

Bixby Creek Bridge is the most-photographed bridge along Highway 1 and the longest concrete arch span in the world, 714′ long and 285′ above Bixby Creek in the steep-walled canyon below. The creek was named after Charlie Bixby, a cousin of President James Knox Polk, who was the first to settle here. Bridge construction used up 6,600 cubic yards of concrete and 600,000 lbs. of reinforcing steel. There are safe observation alcoves on this rainbow bridge which offer a fantastic view of the Pacific. This is another fine vantage point for whale-watching. The sea-lanes are fifteen miles out; with binoculars, you may be able to see a freighter or two.

The ruins at **Castle Rock** at the northern edge of this canyon were the site of old Bixby Landing where Monterey Lime Company, at the turn of the century, transported lime from the ridge by aerial cables to the creek mouth. Depletion of the rich limestone deposit and heavy rains brought the operation to an end after four years. **Robinson Jeffers** used

Bixby Landing as a setting for his narrative poem, *Thurso's Landing*.

In September 1966, Mrs. Lyndon B. Johnson dedicated Highway 1 as California's first Scenic Highway. A plaque was placed at the south end of Bixby Bridge and promptly disappeared, was retrieved and disappeared again. It was inscribed with **Robinson Jeffers'** words:

> "I, gazing at the boundaries of granite and spray,
>   The established sea marks, felt behind me,
> Mountain and plain, the immense breadth of the continent,
>   Before me the mass and doubled stretch of water."

Hurricane Point is the windiest spot on the whole highway, so hang onto your hat! Be extremely careful, especially if you are driving a light car or a top-heavy camper or towing a trailer.

Pico Blanco (elev. 3,710') governs the skyline along the highway past **Little Sur River**. This river was called "Rio Chiquita del Sur" (*Little River of the South*). There is a lovely lagoon where it joins the sea, b this is all private property.

Looming ahead is **Point S Light Station**, built on a gigantic volcanic rock. Before tl lighthouse started warning ships in 1889, many smashed against the treacherous rocks along the coast. During its construction, a steep half-mile road had to be cut into the massive formation for pack mules to climb. With pulleys and ropes, native stone, quarried near Little Sur River, was hoisted. Several small houses and a large stone house, living quarters for the lighthouse keeper and teacher, were also built. The small schoolhouse was 395 steps below the lighthouse. The causeway linking the Station with the mainland used to flood and turn the mighty rock into an island; a sandbar was built to curb the tides.

The elaborate glass prisms, through which the first kerosene lamp was amplified, were made in France and shipped around the horn. This delicately balanced old lamp had to be retired in 1971 because maintenance was costly and time-consuming.

The Navy's dirigible *Macon* broke up and crashed off Point Sur in 1935. Quick action on the part of the lighthouse keeper resulted in the rescue of most of the crew.

Point Sur Light Station now has a powerful million-candlepower light, 50′ above ground and 270′ above sea level, visible for 25 miles. The foghorn blasts every sixty seconds when the coast is obscured. The Station is also equipped with a radio beacon synchronized with six others along the coast.

The Light Station was operated by the U.S. Lighthouse Service until the end of World War II when the U.S. Coast Guard took over. The operation is entirely automated now, so visitors are not allowed. A mini-computer monitor is hooked up with the Coast Guard Station at Monterey, and an electronics technician services the equipment at Point Sur twice a week.

The 2,154 acres of **Andrew Molera State Park**, between Highway 1 and the ocean, extend on both sides of Big Sur River to a point about two miles inland. This property was acquired in 1965, a gift to the State from Miss Frances Molera in memory of her brother. Most of this bucolic acreage will always be maintained in its natural state to preserve its scenic qualities. Picnicking is allowed, but open campfires are not permitted. Hiking trails throughout the park skirt the river or lead to the sea. Surfing and surf-fishing at the mouth of the river and freshwater fishing upstream are allowed.

The old **County Road** goes north out of Andrew Molera State Park over the mountain tops, coming out at the north end of Bixby Creek Bridge on Highway 1. This is a two-lane, hard-packed road, a wooded scenic drive.

Ahead is **Big Sur village**. The residents are a mixture of descendants of early settlers, business people catering to the tourist trade, Park and Forest Service employees, ranchers and farmers, artists, authors, and artisans. This rural community has no mayor and no town hall. Civic matters are settled at meetings held at the Grange Hall, which is also their gathering place for social events, movies, and square dances. The village was slow to acquire civilized amenities enjoyed for many years by Monterey Peninsulans. Electricity didn't reach some homes until 1945. News of the outbreak of World War II was brought by a modern-day Paul Revere on horseback.

Many kinds of accommodations and restaurants are available in the village area, and most are open all year.

Catholic Masses are held every Sunday at **St. Francis of the Redwoods.** This unusual church has a movable glass wall, making it possible to sit indoors or out where amplifiers are hidden in the towering trees. Sunday services are also held year-round at **Santa Lucia Chapel** (Episcopal) in a six-acre redwood grove.

John Pfeiffer was the first permanent white settler at Big Sur. His homestead cabin is in **Pfeiffer Big Sur State Park.** He and his family had planned to find some good farmland farther south, but the winter of 1874 was so severe they were forced to remain in Sycamore Canyon on the west side of the highway. By spring they were settled in and decided to stay.

Pfeiffer Big Sur State Park (2,944 acres) has eighty miles of hiking trails through a sylvan setting watered by Big Sur River. This river is shown on early Spanish maps as "Rio Grande del Sur" (*Big River of the South*). Pfeiffer Park is also the hub for 500 miles of trails through **Los Padres National Forest,** which encompasses 98,000 acres of wilderness. This forest is one of the few places where the Santa Lucia fir (bristlecone fir) grows naturally and is also the southernmost end of the natural range of coast redwoods.

Carmel, Arroyo Seco, Little and Big Sur Rivers run through Ventana Wilderness. There is a 645-mile patchwork of fishing streams with native trout and some with rainbow trout stocked by the State Department of Parks and Recreation.

Two sanctuaries have been established for the California condor, a rare, endangered species; one is in Ventana Wilderness. The most recent count showed only thirty-six of these huge birds, with wing spans up to 9½', still exist. The condor is the largest North American land bird and nests only every other year. The female lays a single egg, not in a nest but in soft earth in sandstone cliffs or bluffs.

Point Sur

Deer, wild boar, and an occasional black bear inhabit the forest, as well as numerous smaller animals. Grizzly bears were plentiful in Monterey County at one time. Now the State Department of Fish and Game estimates there are between twelve and fifteen bears in the County, most in Los Padres National Forest.

Pfeiffer Big Sur State Park is a popular spot for outdoor enjoyment, a favorite of campers, and always crowded in summer months and on good-weather weekends throughout the year. There is a day-use fee and campsite charges. Hundreds of campers are turned away, so reserve early. Reservations can be made by contacting any California State Park office. There are developed campsites, trailer facilities, group campsites, picnic areas, swimming and fishing in the river, and riding and hiking trails. Guided nature walks and outdoor community programs on summer evenings are among the many nature-geared activities at the Park.

Below Pfeiffer cabin is the rock-rimmed gravesite of the last Indian family to live at Big Sur. **Mt. Manuel** was named after Immanuel (Manuel) Innocenti, who was a vaquero for Juan Bautista Cooper, owner of Rancho El Sur. On a clear day, Mt. Manuel is the goal of many hikers. The trail climbs 4½ miles to an elevation of 3,100' for a splendid view of the coastline on one side and the vast wilderness on the other. Another trail leads to **Pfeiffer Falls** through a cathedral-like grove of stately coast redwoods.

Another path leads down to white, sandy **Pfeiffer Beach** and lagoon and its sea-carved caves. Take your coat; it's usually very gusty here. Busy sandpipers scurry back and forth eluding the tide. *The Sandpiper*, starring Elizabeth Taylor and Richard Burton, was filmed on this beach.

Big Sur Lodge is a State concession with hotel-type accommodations and housekeeping cottages, dining room, coffee shop, gift shop, and general store.

Fire permits, camping information, and forest regulations are available at **Big Sur Guard Station**, ¼ mile south of the State Park entrance. If you intend to hike into Ventana Wilderness, you must sign in here.

Big Sur's first post office and first school district were at **Post Hill**, another bustling way station on the road from Monterey. William B. Post from Connecticut was responsible for founding the small community in 1877. The renovated Post Homestead, one thousand feet above sea level, is a reminder of those early days.

Nepenthe is defined as *a potion used in ancient times to* *drown pain and sorrow.* The steep path from the parking lot is worth the climb to view the seascape from the modern-day Nepenthe, 808' above sea level. This was originally a log house built by the Trails Club many years ago. Orson Welles once purchased it as a castle for his movie queen, Rita Hayworth, but she preferred the Aga Khan and never lived there.

The sandy beach at **Castro Canyon** is populated by sea lions. They bask in the sun and splash in the surf. Don't try going down the cliff; the rescue patrol will probably have to haul you up!

Stop on the oceanside across from **Grimes Canyon**. You may hear the barking of a huge herd of seals 700' below. This is another sheer drop-off, so be careful.

Many years ago Harry Lafler, a former editor, made his home in the hollowed-out trunk of a redwood tree at **Lafler Canyon** and later in a one-room house built from marble quarried from his land. Now two round redwood tanks house an art gallery on this site.

Drive carefully over **Torre Canyon Bridge**; the curves are sharp. The cluster of mailboxes on the road belong to families living atop **Partington Ridge**. John Partington was aboard the *S.S. Venture* when it wrecked off Point Sur in 1879, strewing its cargo of wagons and linens along the coast. He decided to settle on this ridge and make a living by hauling tanbark and timber.

Jaime de Angulo, cowboy, anthropologist, medical doctor, professor, and author, lived on Partington Ridge in the 1920s and '30s. He shared the beauties of his land in death as he did in life. **De Angulo Trail** was bequeathed to the U.S. Forest Service and leads to the top of Partington Ridge for a great view of the raw coastline. It is three miles to Coast Ridge Road, four miles to Cold Springs Camp and nine miles to the south fork of Big Sur River. This is a mountainous trail and should be attempted by experienced hikers only.

At peaceful **Julia Pfeiffer Burns State Park** (1,725 acres), only the parking and picnic areas and trail to the headland are open to the public. Some of the ridges within the Park rise to 3,000'. A steep path leads to a small beach at the mouth of the creek, another to the old tanbark dock. A pedestrian underpass goes to a spot overlooking the waterfall at **Saddle Rock** where McWay Creek plummets 50' into the ocean. A 2½-square-mile offshore underwater reserve protects marine life in the area. Experienced diving groups may get permission at Big Sur Guard Station to dive along this part of the coast.

In pioneer days this park was Saddle Rock Ranch, owned in more recent years by Lathrop Brown. The **tin house** high above the fog line was supposed to have been built for Franklin D. Roosevelt as a quiet retreat for writing his memoirs after his term as President. Brown, who was Roosevelt's lifelong friend, constructed the unusual house in the early 1940s with materials from three abandoned gas stations. Unfortunately, the President did not live long enough to write his story in the "tin house."

California State law made prisoners available for highway work on a paid basis. Some of the convicts who helped build Highway 1 lived in shacks near Anderson Creek and Kirk Creek to the south. From here work proceeded in both directions. Later **Anderson Landing** became an art colony. In the mid-forties Henry Miller, famed author, and Emil White, painter of primitives, lived here.

Located at **Old Slate's Hot Springs** overlooking the Pacific is **Esalen Institute**, known nation-wide for its programs to expand human potential. The sign at the front gate reads "By Reservation Only," which, loosely translated, probably means "Keep Out."

John Little State Reserve (21 acres) is open for daytime use but has no facilities as yet. Fog hangs over this spot in the summertime; when clear, however, the view of the coast is tremendous.

At least 700 years ago the Esselens probably watched Cabrillo and Vizcaíno making their way up the coast to explore California. Diggings have shown that an Indian village with a population of about 100 flourished near Big Creek

Bridge. Nature Conservancy has been responsible for preserving the 4,000-acre **Big Creek Ranch**, which spreads for four miles along the coast and reaches up 6,000' to the highlands of the Santa Lucia Mountains. One of the southernmost stands of redwood trees in the world is here, plus a pristine watershed, natural springs, several streams, and a remarkable diversity of plant life and an equally diverse wildlife population. The ranch has been transferred to the University of California for use as an outdoor laboratory for teaching and research in ecological and biological studies.

The highway curls south to **Gamboa Point, Lopez Point,** and the little town of **Lucia** where Wilbur and Ada Harlan homesteaded in 1885. These self-reliant settlers raised ten children, and members of the third generation of the Harlan family still live at Lucia.

A mosaic sign by the roadway marks the entrance to the only American branch of the Benedictine Order. This is the former Lucia Ranch, 1,300' above sea level in the Santa Lucia Mountains. **New Camaldoli Immaculate Heart Hermitage** was established in 1958 in a setting much like that of the original Order founded in the eleventh century in the Appenines near Florence, Italy. Outsiders rarely see any of the gentle Camaldolese monks who are dedicated to a hermitlike life of prayer and creative and scholarly duties. Visitors are welcome to attend twice-daily Masses in the chapel. The anteroom is a little shop, run by volunteers, with religious artifacts and books, plus carvings and artworks made by the monks. Delicious brandied fruitcake is made in the Hermitage kitchen year-round and is sold here and at the Hermitage Shop in Carmel.

While Highway 1 was under construction, 163,000 yards of rock had to be removed every 1,000' to curve the road around **Limekiln Point**. The bridge here spans a beautiful natural canyon with a waterfall. In the late 1800s schooners picked up bricks from Rockland Cement Company's four large limekilns at the mouth of the creek. An easy half-mile walk will take you there. A short side trip off the same path leads to the waterfall. Jasper and iron pyrite can be found along this creek and occasionally poor quality agates and garnets.

There are good campsites, trailer spaces, and a picnic area on bluffs overlooking the ocean at **Kirk Creek Campground**, operated by the U.S. Forest Service.

From the south end of Kirk Creek Bridge, **Nacimiento Grade** winds and climbs to nearly 4,000' and then down to **Jolon** in the San Antonio Valley, about thirty miles. This is a narrow, asphalt-paved, scenic road. The highway leading out of Jolon goes to **King City** (twenty miles) on U.S. Highway 101. The Portolá expedition camped in San Antonio Valley in 1769, and in 1771 Padre Junipero Serra founded the third California Mission here, **San Antonio de Padua**, which eventually became one of the richest and most populous of the chain as hundreds of Indians were converted. At the outbreak of World War II, the Federal Government purchased thousands of acres of land adjacent to the Mission from William Randolph Hearst to establish **Hunter Liggett Military Reservation**. Hearst's holdings extended from his hunting lodge, now Hunter Liggett's headquarters, to fabled **Hearst Castle** at **San Simeon** to the south of Big Sur.

Pacific Valley is bordered by Wild Cattle Creek on the north and Prewitt Creek on the south. This is a four-mile stretch of rather level road, and access to the beach is easy for surf-anglers and skindivers.

By crossing the field beyond the parking lot at **Sand Dollar Picnic Area** and descending the stairs, you will reach a lovely, crescent-shaped beach. Watch for hang gliders on the bluffs; they are here nearly every weekend.

Just offshore you'll see a huge rock that, to early Spanish travelers, appeared to have rather feminine contours. They were the ones who gave the little town of **Gorda**, the last stop on the Big Sur mail run, its name. "Gorda" means *fat lady*. At this writing, this lively little ghost town is for sale. About twenty people live on the nine-acre site; they work in the restaurant, store, or service station. A cluster of cabins appeared in the 1930s when the State began pushing the highway south to San Simeon, but the history of the area goes way back. The region took its place in the State's history in 1875 when the Los Burros Mining District was formed. The discovery of the Coastal Mother Lode prompted the filing of over two thousand claims. However, Los Burros never really boomed, probably because of the difficulties in bringing ore out of the rugged terrain. Hundreds of thousands of dollars' worth of gold were taken out before the era ended. If Gorda is sold for the asking price of $950,000., it will be the biggest strike ever reported in the Los Burros District.

Plaskett Creek has another U.S. Forest Service campground with trailer and camping facilities, and about a quarter of a mile south, you can park and take the stairs down to Jade Cove's rocky beach.

Jade Cove has produced perhaps a million dollars' worth of quality nephrite jade in rare blue/green colors. Fine Pacific Blue Jade, found nowhere else in the world, is worth over $200. a pound. Prize specimens of this color are sought by collectors world over. In 1971, a 9,000-lb. hunk of nephrite jade, 8½' long and 5' high, and worth $180,000., was dredged from beneath 30' of water near Jade Cove. *The Guinness Book of Records* lists it as the largest piece of jade ever found. Rockhounds have been busy here for many years, but it is still possible to find small pieces of jade on the beach and in the serpentine cliffs at this cove. Skindivers can bring up larger pieces. Most jade found nowadays is the common green and black serpentine and far from the real thing. The best specimens are found at low tide or after a winter storm. **Willow Creek** is an easy place to go down to the south end of Jade Cove where you can look for bits of jade stirred up by washing waves.

An easily overlooked dirt road leads to **Cape San Martin**. This is a good whale-watching spot, but the road is often impassable during winter months.

Just south of Willow Creek, a narrow dirt road leads up to **Los Burros Mining District**. Mining roads are steep, rough, dusty, dry, and dangerous; a four-wheel drive vehicle is need-

CARMEL

Pt. Lobos

Palo
Colorado Rd.

Rocky Point

ROCKY POINT
RESTAURANT

Big Sur Country

THE
CARMEL
MISSION

Little Sur River

Point
Sur

Molera Park
River Inn
Big Sur Campground
Riverside Campground
Whispering Pines
Fernwood
Pfeiffer Beach
Big Sur Bazaar
Loma Vista
Nepenthe

Big Sur River

Surtreks
Ripplewood
Glen Oaks Motel

Big Sur Lodge

Pfeiffer Big Sur State Park
U.S. Forest Service
Ventano
Deetjens Big Sur Inn

Coast Gallery
Julia Pfeiffer Burns Park

BIG LODGE SUR

NEPENTHE
PHOENIX SHOP

Esalen

PACIFIC OCEAN

VENTANA

Lucia Lodge

Limekiln Creek
Redwoods Campground
Kirk
Creek

Nacimianto Rd.

Mill
Creek

Pacific Valley

Hearst
Castle

Sand dollar
Beach

Cape
St. Martin

26 miles to Hearst Castle

Gorda

ed. The District stretches from Plaskett Ridge south to San Carpoforo Creek. Most of the land west of Hunter Liggett is open to prospecting and mining exploration, except private claims. Do not explore, prospect, hunt, or fish on land that may be inhabited. Mining claims may not be clearly marked, but trespassing is met sternly.

After leaving the mother lode in California's Gold Country, a few Chinese began exploring along the creeks in San Antonio Valley. They found a little gold, continued west and eventually returned to their ancestral occupation, fishing. Around 1855 gold-bearing gravels were found in the westerly Santa Lucia Mountains, and many more miners moved in. Los Burros Mining District was formed by these miners in the 1870s. The District still produces small amounts of gold, silver, chromium, jade, and quicksilver. Every element known in the earth's crust and almost every geological condition is found in a small way somewhere in these high mountains. Even platinum has been found in the streams. A few present-day prospectors are seeking the legendary pot of gold; they work the old mines and skillfully recover tiny amounts of precious metals or hunt for large jade deposits near the coast.

Salmon Creek waterfall is a few miles north of the Monterey County line and is in the southernmost stand of sequoia redwoods. Hardy hikers can clamber up the creek, climb behind the falls, and get a damp, but delightful view through cascading water. This is an important steelhead trout spawning area. From the first heavy rains in the fall through January, steelhead spawn in most of the large creeks to the north, too.

Highway 1 wends southward to San Simeon and Hearst Castle, sixty-seven miles from the Big Sur Post Office. You have traveled through incomparable Big Sur country, and you will do so again because Big Sur always beckons. As **Lillian Bos Ross** mused: "Perhaps Big Sur is not a country at all, only a state of mind."

7.
Flourishing
Seaside

■ Seaside owes its existence to Dr. John L. D. Roberts, who came to the Monterey Peninsula in 1887 with only a brand new diploma from New York University's Medical School and a single silver dollar in his pocket. He bought a 160-acre ranch on what is now Seaside and Sand City from his uncle for $5,000. on credit and filed a butcher paper map as his claim to the title. Within a year after subdividing the land, he had paid for it in full, had money in the bank, owned his own home and had 1,000 additional building lots to sell in what was then called "East Monterey." He founded the Seaside Post Office in 1890, and Seaside was born. He, and his wife later, acted as postmaster for forty-two years.

Dr. Roberts became a familiar figure making house calls on horseback along the Big Sur coast, all the while charting the wilderness and dreaming of the day when there would be a highway. He saw that dream realized in 1937 when Highway 1 was dedicated.

In 1897 this remarkable man made a five-day trip on foot from San Luis Obispo to Monterey and mapped the rugged country in between. Eighteen years later he stood before the California legislature showing colored slides on a bed sheet and describing this magnificent area he loved so much. As a result, the State earmarked $1½ million for building another highway.

In the twenty years the doctor served on the Monterey

County Board of Supervisors, four of them as chairman, he never missed a meeting. He saw that the Presidio of Monterey was enlarged and rebuilt in 1902 and pioneered the building of Highway 1 between Monterey and Castroville. A fitting memorial to this outdoorsman of vision is **Roberts Lake** in Seaside where youngsters of all ages enjoy remote-control boating.

Seaside is bounded on the north and east by Fort Ord, Del Rey Oaks on the south, Monterey on the west, and Sand City and Monterey Bay on the northwest. The city's slogan is: "Seaside means business!" It is the fastest growing residential and commercial community on the Monterey Peninsula with a population over 40,000, five times its pre-World War II size.

The city has made great strides in overcoming its early image of a wide-open town of the new frontier. Seaside grew haphazardly until its incorporation in 1954. Speculators took their money and moved on, leaving the land little improved. Squatters built shacks and settled in the sand dunes and sagebrush and didn't bother to plant trees. During depression years lots sold for as little as one dollar. The *San Francisco Chronicle* offered free lots in Seaside as a come-on for new subscribers, few of whom ever settled here.

With the start of World War II and the establishment of the huge Fort Ord complex, land values rose. Since then an extensive urban renewal program has helped to replace substandard homes with hundreds of new homes in the growing residential areas overlooking the Peninsula skyline and Monterey Bay. Many military and civilian personnel from Fort Ord and the Naval Postgraduate School make their homes here. The citizens of Seaside are proud of their city's international character; nearly every country in the world is represented among its residents.

Seaside City Hall, on a 5 1/3-acre site at 440 Harcourt Avenue, was designed by world-renowned architect Edward Durell Stone. A continuous and changing showing of art works is on display here. Hours are 8 A.M.–5 P.M., closed Saturday and Sunday.

The **Monterey Peninsula Buddhist Temple** at 1155 Noche Buena is an unexpected and appreciated sight. A latticed gate leads into a large compound of Oriental loveliness with its classic gardens, water falling into a pond full of carp, and to the glass-sided buildings beyond. English-speaking services are held Sundays at 10:15 A.M. First, second and third generation Japanese (Isei, Nisei and Sensei) sponsor the two-day **Obon Festival** at the Monterey County Fairgrounds in July, and an **Annual Bonsai Show** is held in the Temple in May.

St. Seraphim's Russian Orthodox Church was built in the early 1950s on the site of Seaside's first post office, but has since been moved to Canyon Del Rey and Frances Avenue on the shores of Laguna Del Rey. It is worth driving by to see the church's Slavic architecture.

Seaside has an unusual university, the first of its kind in the United States. **The Academy of Arts and Humanities**, 1137 Broadway, was independently established without aid from foundations or governmental agencies. Based on a structure which predates the medieval university, the school has revived the ancient format of an academy. Students learn, not only in classrooms, but individually and in small groups in the studios of accomplished professionals. They are encouraged to create and produce in their fields and market the results. The curriculum includes performing arts, fine arts, classics, history, philosophy, religions, mathematics, comparative literature, languages, marriage counseling, and Asian, Black and Semitic studies. The Academy has been qualified by the California State Superintendent of Education and two-year diplomas are granted.

Urban Redevelopment programs have made Seaside a forerunner for cities of its size. Among four renewal projects is the **Monterey Peninsula Auto Center**, a contemporary concept in new car shopping. It is a nine-dealer complex built around meandering pedestrian malls.

David Cutino Park (five acres) at Noche Buena and San Pablo Avenues has playground equipment, a full-sized athletic field, picnic area with barbecue pits and a multiuse court for tennis, basketball, and volleyball.

An eight-foot-wide, paved **pedestrian–equestrian–bicycle trail** starts at the northern edge of Seaside's city limits, running along the west side of the freeway, and goes to Fort Ord's main gate near Gigling Road where there is a vista point with a fine view of Monterey Bay. From there this $94,000. path leads all the way to Marina. This is the longest bike trail in the state and first to be built next to a freeway.

8.
Close-By
Communities

DEL REY OAKS

In a sun pocket sandwiched between Monterey and Seaside, nestled in a grove of oak trees, is the quiet residential community of Del Rey Oaks. Since its incorporation in 1953, the 2,000 residents have carefully preserved the family quality of Del Rey Oaks. All but four lots are zoned for single-family homes.

In the middle of the 286 wooded acres, on the floor of Canyon Del Rey, is a 34-acre park. The stream running through the canyon feeds Laguna Del Rey and Roberts Lake. Facilities include a recreation building, golf driving range, tennis courts, and a ball field, all built with aid from the Bing Crosby Youth Fund.

SAND CITY

Sand City is wedged between Seaside and Monterey Bay in the rolling dunes on the shoreside of the railroad tracks. It has the distinction of being the second smallest incorporated city in the state and is described as "a mile wide and a mile-and-a-half long." Sand City has a residential population of approximately 500, but nearly 2,000 workers are employed in its commercial and light industrial establishments.

Canyon as yet inaccessible to general public
provides untapped fishing hole

117

The dunes along Highway 1 adjacent to Sand City are the gathering place of the California Condors, Monterey Bay's hang-glider enthusiasts. You can watch these adventurous sportsmen sky-surf off the sandy cliffs nearly every weekend.

FORT ORD

Fort Ord was named after Maj. Gen. Edward Otho Cresap Ord, a famed Indian fighter who served as a lieutenant under Gen. John C. Fremont, commanded the first U.S. Army garrison at the Presidio of Monterey and later distinguished himself as a combat officer in the Civil War.

In 1917 the Federal Government purchased 15,324 acres of sand dunes and scrub oaks near the present East Garrison for only $1.04 an acre. This land was known as Gigling Reservation, named after a German family who once lived in the area; Gigling Road still bears their name. At first the base, which consisted of a caretaker's house and a few bivouac sites, was used as a training ground for the old 11th Cavalry and 76th Artillery, both stationed at the Presidio. Then it remained dormant for many years except when National Guard and Army Reserve units trained in the summertime.

Twenty-thousand acres were added in 1940, and Camp Ord became Fort Ord, a permanent Army base. The 7th Infantry was reactivated under the command of Gen. Joseph W. Stilwell and became the first major unit to occupy the post. During World War II years, Fort Ord was a staging and training area averaging about 35,000 troops; at one time there were more than 50,000. The amphibians who made thirty invasions, including the reconquest of the Philippines, were trained here. Basic training was also provided for recruits for the Korean and Vietnam wars.

Today Fort Ord encompasses 28,500 acres. Satellite operations include the 286,000-acre Hunter Liggett Military Reservation, 70 miles south, and 44,000-acre Camp Roberts, 90 miles south on Highway 101.

Once again the late "Vinegar Joe's" outfit has returned. Fort Ord has changed from its role as a basic training base to permanent brigade headquarters for the 7th Infantry. The reservation is home for nearly 20,000 Army personnel attached to four infantry battalions, a field artillery battalion, brigade headquarters, headquarters company and selected support units. The 2nd Squadron of the 10th Air Cavalry has 30 helicopters assigned to reconnaissance and security.

An estimated 16,500 retired military from all branches of the armed services and their dependents use Fort Ord's facilities. Over 3,500 civilians are employed here. Installations at the base include service clubs, libraries, theaters, craft shops, exchanges, indoor and outdoor sports facilities, chapels, and a 440-bed hospital that you can see on the skyline.

If you are curious about the red flags flying on the bayside of the highway, they indicate that the infantrymen are practicing on the target ranges.

MARINA

Sand from the dunes around present-day Marina was used as a primary source for rebuilding much of San Francisco following the disastrous 1906 earthquake and fire. Other than that, Sand Hill Ranch, as the area was known, produced only potatoes in those days.

William Locke Paddon, a San Francisco land promoter with faith in the future, bought 1,500 acres of arid wasteland inhabited by rattlesnakes, ground squirrels, jack rabbits and coyotes. Today there are many who wish they could have purchased property for $20. an acre in the heart of Marina as Paddon did in 1915. The little undeveloped land left in the Monterey Peninsula's third largest city now sells for hundreds of times that figure.

Paddon subdivided his desolate property into five-acre parcels and brought clients from San Francisco aboard the Southern Pacific for expense-paid weekends in "Paddonville," as the railroad company called it. The only greenery was in a sparse garden around the caretaker's old shack. Paddon was asking for $75. an acre with $10 down, but buyers weren't too interested, so he was forced to sell on almost any terms, even $5. a month. The few who did settle were presented with cypress seedlings; some of the trees still form windbreaks on the dunes. The first residents, mostly French, eked out a living by growing potatoes, peas, turnips, and cabbages.

Not many people liked the name "Paddonville," so in 1920 it was changed to "Marina," but otherwise the town changed little until after World War II when housing was needed for families of soldiers stationed at Fort Ord. The population doubled and redoubled several times. In the late fifties subdivisions grew, and now there are acres of homes, hundreds of apartments, and five mobile home parks which house 24,000 residents. There are also six shopping areas and six schools. No longer a "bedroom community" for Fort Ord, incorporated Marina is the "Gateway to the Monterey Peninsula."

Marina has a five-acre park on the knoll to the right of the highway, off Vista Del Sur near Susan Avenue. Barbecue pits and picnic tables are available.

Salinas River State Beach, a few miles north of Marina, is undeveloped, but you can play in the huge sand dunes or on the beach which extends almost to Moss Landing. To reach it, take Potrero Road off Highway 1.

9.

Castroville,
the Artichoke Capital

■ Juan Bautista Castro, who was born in Monterey in 1835, inherited almost 40,000 acres from his wealthy and distinguished family. His father, Simeon C. Castro, was the first Alcalde (mayor) of Monterey under Mexican rule, and his mother was the sister of California's last governor under Mexican rule. Young Castro realized that the area's future depended on attracting and encouraging new settlers. He subdivided his land into large ranches and donated property for a townsite, which he named "Castroville."

By 1875 this second oldest town in Monterey County was flourishing with a population of 1,000. Southern Pacific had a right-of-way and passengers ate a hurried lunch at the new hotel while the train's crew changed. The County's first hospital was built, and Wells Fargo established an office. The new brewery spawned thirteen saloons.

Don Juan Bautista, as Castro was known, presided over the community and was among the last of the California Dons. Unwise investments eventually left him nearly penniless. He endured failing health in his waning years and died in 1915. His simple gravesite is in the small cemetery that he donated to the town many years before.

When Southern Pacific moved its main line east to Salinas, Castroville was nearly forgotten. The population dwindled to only a few hundred. Even so, some Spanish land grant holders in the area did not sell out. Descendants of the Cooper and

Molera families still own portions of original grants. At the turn of the century, most of the rich acreage was planted in potatoes and wheat. In the early 1900s, it was hoped that chicken farming would revive the economy, but this plan, too, laid an egg. Finally it was an edible thistle that saved Castroville. Because of the globe artichoke (*Cynara scolymus*), a member of the sunflower family, the population of Castroville now tops 9,500.

According to an Aegean legend, the first artichoke was a lovely young maiden who lived on the Island of Zinari. Envious of her beauty, an angry god changed her into an artichoke. The story of the artichoke industry in Castroville is a modern-day legend.

The first globe artichokes in America were planted by the French in Louisiana and Florida and by the Spanish in California. They are native to North Africa and the Mediterranean region. In fact, the Pharaohs dined on artichokes, as proved by hieroglyphics found in Egyptian pyramids. Italian immigrants brought the crop to Half Moon Bay north of San Francisco. Flat farmland was scarce there, so in the 1920s these farmers began buying and leasing as much land as possible around Castroville. Artichokes need Castroville's ideal growing conditions—rich, fast-draining soil, cool, foggy summers, and mild winters. Today a fifteen-mile radius of picturesque, precision-planted artichoke fields frames the town.

A weather-beaten sign spans Castroville's main street proclaiming it "The Artichoke Center of the World." It exaggerates; Italy, France and Spain out-produce Castroville, but it can claim fame as the "artichoke heart" of the United States.

About 10,500 acres are devoted to the cultivation of globe artichokes in this area, and Castroville produces ninety percent of the country's crop. Most of the growers are Italian, and the field and plant workers are Mexican-American for the most part. Eighty-five percent of the crop is shipped fresh throughout the country. Speed is the secret of successfully trimming and quick-freezing this delicate vegetable. The rest of the crop is processed in several plants.

Annually six million jars of marinated artichokes are shipped out of Castroville. Only a few hours elapse between the time they are picked from the dewy fields in the morning until they are packed into jars and stored in warehouses. The recipe for the spicy oil marinade has been handed down from generation to generation by Italian families.

Planting of artichokes takes place in the summer and fall. They produce within six months, depending on sunshine and rain. From then on they are picked every five to ten days and are normally through producing in May. With a pruning process called "stumping," the plants will bear again within 100 days. Without man's help, artichokes would be available only four months of the year. New planting takes place every seven years. The peak production season is during April and May. Winter-kissed artichokes with their bronze-tipped outer leaves are available during December, January and February.

Experiments to improve the artichoke crop, under the direction of the Artichoke Research Association, are constant. Much hand labor is required for cultivation and harvesting, which makes artichokes less profitable than other row crops. Local plants are being cross-bred with species from Argentina, Chile, Italy, France, Spain, and Greece. Artichokes are perennial, taking two years to develop seeds, and often revert to their wild state when grown in this manner. Botanists are experimenting with cuttings, as well as seeds, replanting those with desirable traits. The goal of this ten-year research project is to develop the ultimate artichoke—a small plant of uniform size with a high density of production, resistant to frost and the plume moth, a machine-harvestable strain.

Roadside stands have morning-picked artichokes year-round and fresh mushrooms, too. Some will ship artichokes anywhere for you, and all have free recipes for preparing them in various ways. Sizes range from peewee, suitable for marinating and barbecuing; medium for individual servings; and large for stuffing for entrées.

If not picked, artichokes become huge and handsome

Castroville's Great Artichoke

purple flowers. These dried blooms, for use in floral arrangements, are also available at some stands.

Castroville's **Annual Artichoke Festival** is held the first weekend of September to herald the fall crop. Aside from having a good time, the purpose is to call attention to the artichoke and its many delicious uses.

Marilyn Monroe, then a budding actress, came to Castroville in 1947 to be crowned "California Artichoke Queen." The local movie house, coincidentally, was showing a double bill: *Carnival in Costa Rica* and *Backlash*. Miss Monroe had bit parts in both films.

10.
Moss Landing,
the Snug Harbor

■ Moss Landing's beginning dates back to shortly before the Civil War. At that time Paul Lezere, a Frenchman, purchased 300 acres from the State of California for $300. and plotted a dream city which he vainly called "City of St. Paul." A ferry was installed across Elkhorn Slough, now spanned by the highway bridge, and Legere started selling land. A few people bought lots, varying in price from $40. to $600., but none ever built homes, so Lezere sold out in 1871 to Cato Vierra, a whaling captain from the Portuguese Azores, who replaced the ferry with a toll bridge. Members of the same Vierra family live near this original land.

When Captain Charles Moss, a Texan with foresight and determination, arrived on the scene, he envisioned an opportunity to develop the port to handle large shipments of grain grown in the Pajaro and Salinas valleys. Together Moss and Vierra built a wharf, and the first ship to sail out of the new port carried 100 tons of wheat which hired men had to carry on their backs through waist-deep water, load on surf boats and transfer to the ship. Soon the port became known as "Moss's Landing," later shortened to "Moss Landing."

Steamers, carrying dairy products, cured meats and hides, stopped regularly on their way to San Francisco. On return trips they brought early settlers to the two agricultural valleys. In 1874 the Southern Pacific line was extended to Watsonville and slough traffic diminished, although barge traffic continued for another fifteen years.

Captain Moss left his namesake town for San Francisco with a quarter of a million dollars. Amid the early-day photographs hanging on the walls of the tiny renovated Moss Landing Post Office is a sign offering a $5. reward for a picture of Captain Moss.

Between 1917 and 1927, folks didn't have to ask directions to Moss Landing; they followed their noses! A whaling station had been established on the island and as many as five whales a week were hauled in. During prohibition Moss Landing was a haven for rumrunners who brought contraband liquor from Canada.

The whales departed for better waters, and the sardines arrived. After the depression Moss Landing's economy skyrocketed as purse seiners brought in hundreds of tons of sardines nightly. The little fish disappeared in the mid-forties, as they did at Monterey, leaving the district desperate for funds. Sometimes there was barely enough to pay utility bills.

While the establishment of Moss Landing's industries improved district finances, they are sometimes lauded and sometimes lamented. Pacific Gas and Electric Company's steam generating plant, the second largest of its kind in the world, with its tall towers and myriad of bright lights, has been dubbed "Mighty Moss." Kaiser Refractories, by a very complex operation, manufactures basic refractory brick used in high-temperature furnaces in steel, glass, and cement industries. Since their establishment, however, Moss Landing's citizens, who now number 650, have reconsidered their industrial future. Seriously concerned about pollution of all kinds, they set up rigid restrictions for industries wanting to locate here. Moss Landing is not likely to become a huge industrial complex; boats are Moss Landing's real business.

The Army Corps of Engineers built the sea channel in 1946. It is 200' wide with an entrance 15' deep and runs from the sand dunes at the tip of Monterey Bay's submarine canyon to the inner harbor. The canyon is at the seaward end of the entrance to the channel and has a calming effect on adjacent waters even during roughest storms. Moss Landing's

T-shaped harbor, which is 1,500 yards long and 200 yards wide, stretches from Elkhorn Yacht Club to Sandholt Bridge. It has long been considered the safest refuge between Los Angeles and San Francisco; skippers say they can "tie their boats with a shoestring."

More than three hundred fishing boats are moored in the basin during off-season months. Each morning dozens puff out in search of salmon, tuna, albacore, and other large fish. On the west side of the highway is **Elkhorn Yacht Club** where over a hundred handsome sailboats and cruisers are tied up.

Moss Landing Marine Laboratories on Sandholt Road is a federally funded National Sea Grant College operated by six campuses of the state university and college system and the University of California. Graduate students study marine biology, oceanography, and related subjects, hoping to bridge the gap between industrial and conservation interests. A 102' steel-hulled former Navy tug, named *Oconostota* after an Indian chief, serves as a floating laboratory. Open house is held at the Laboratories in April.

International Shellfish Enterprises of California is the first venture of its kind on the Pacific Coast. Eastern blue point oysters are cultivated in the warm effluent from Pacific Gas and Electric's generating plant. Larvae are placed in tanks of sterile sea water in the hatchery room where they are force-fed algae and introduced to the warm waste water. When they reach ½" in size, they are transferred to the tank farm and kept until 2" in size. After nine months the oysters are moved to holding trays in the "grow-out" area in the slough for nature to fatten them up. Within twelve to fifteen months from their start, the oysters are ready to be shipped to market for serving on the half-shell. Abalone, clams and scallops are also being grown by this new aquaculture process.

Turn down Moss Landing Road and plan to spend a few hours seeing this seagoing town. All the stores have free maps of Moss Landing and vicinity, courtesy of the chamber of commerce, so pick one up at your first stop.

You can find anything from buttons to bureaus in this

antique browsers' paradise. Whatever you're looking for, you will probably find it in one of Moss Landing's shops with delightful names. Pirate Cove Flea Market, across the bridge, has various kinds of shops under one roof, open every day in the summertime and Thursday through Sunday in the winter. That's a one-way bridge to the island, and the natives are determined to keep it. Who else can boast about owning a one-way bridge?

Moss Landing has all kinds of fishing, from party boats or small boats, from the docks, from the shore inside the harbor, or from the jetties. Shore fishing is good at the mouth of the **Pajaro River** at **Zmudowski State Beach** (156 acres), down Giberson Road. This is a day-use park for swimming, picnicking and fishing. Fishing licenses are available at the liquor store. (Where else?)

You can dig pismo clams in season at this beach, too, and there's gaper and Washington clamming on the slough's muddy edges at **Jetty State Beach** (55 acres), off Jetty Road. Be careful; the tide and undertow are very tricky.

Moss Landing's original marshland eventually became the salt works, **Monterey Salt Company**, north of Elkhorn Slough, which has been in operation since the middle of the nineteenth century. Salt water is drawn into ponds and passes through five evaporating beds before it becomes pure salt. Some of the ponds are also used for raising brine shrimp for bait. The pinky-white mountain of salt is surrounded by tidepools and swamps which are a nesting ground for many birds and a favorite of birdwatchers.

Elkhorn Slough, California's first **Federal Estuarine Sanctuary**, serves as an important link in the coastal flyway for migratory shore birds and waterfowl. These wetlands are a feeding trough and resting place for the endangered clapper rail, a small chicken-like coastal bird, and for grebes, terns, loons, mallards, ducks, curlew, pelicans, pheasants, pigeons, sandpipers, gulls, whistling swans, godwits, willets, herons, and egrets, more than ninety species in all who sometimes visit 20,000 at a time. There are also two unlikely permanent settlers, a pair of exotic flame-colored flamingoes whose native habitat is in the Caribbean. The birds share the slough with seventy species of fish and shellfish, plus harbor seals, sea otters, and raccoons. No powerboats are allowed in the winding canals, just canoes, kayaks, and rowboats. The Sierra Club has estimated that over 30,000 persons every year use the slough as a source of quiet recreation – photography, bird-watching, and observing many kinds of wildlife.

By now you have fallen in love with Moss Landing and the friendly folks who live here, so come back for their **Shark Derby** in late May and early June, the **Flea Market** in July or the **Annual Festival and Fish Fry** in August, or join in the fun at the community **Hallowe'en Parade and Party**.

11.
Helpful
ℂ Sightseeing Services

Monterey's **PATH OF HISTORY** is a well-marked, self-guided, 2.7-mile tour of 46 historic buildings, including the **Custom House, Colton Hall, Robert Louis Stevenson House, California's First Theatre,** the **Old Whaling Station,** and other sites rich in the area's history. Some have curators on duty and are open to the public; others are private offices and homes. A few of the historic buildings require small entrance fees. Free maps are available at the **Monterey History and Art Association,** 412 Pacific St. or 550 Calle Principal, Monterey, and at the **Monterey Peninsula Chamber of Commerce,** 380 Alvarado, Monterey, or at their **Visitors Information Center** at Camino El Estero and Webster, Monterey. Allow at least 2 hours if walking and 1½ hours if driving. Follow the red-orange line.

CALIFORNIA HERITAGE GUIDES provide an enjoyable way to explore Monterey. Four walking tours, conducted by qualified guides, are offered nearly every day year-round: Tour No. 1, Robert Louis Stevenson House area; Tour No. 2, Custom House Plaza area; Tour No. 3, Monterey Town House and Old Jail area; and Tour No. 4, Cannery Row. The average tour lasts 1½–2 hours. Admission fees per tour are inexpensive and include entrance fees to historic buildings where required. Reservations are necessary. Individually guided tours

First brick building

anywhere on the Monterey Peninsula are also available, as well as custom-designed motor tours, using your car or theirs. California Heritage Guides' office is at 10 Custom House Plaza, Monterey.

A free guide, GALLERY TOUR OF CARMEL-BY-THE-SEA, including a good map of the village, is available at all Carmel galleries and from major hotels and motels on the Monterey Peninsula.

SURTREKS at Big Sur sponsors guided nature walks in Big Sur State Parks for exploring the redwood groves, beaches, bluffs, and rivers. Groups are limited to 12 persons per walk for adults and children over 8. These are 3-4-hour treks conducted by trained guides and leave mornings and afternoons from respective parks. Reservations are required.

AIRPLANE RENTALS

Del Monte Aviation, Inc., Monterey Peninsula Airport, Monterey

Monarch Aviation, Inc., Monterey Peninsula Airport, Monterey

AUTOMOBILE RENTALS

American Auto Rental & Sales Co., Inc., Monterey Peninsula Airport or 801 Airport Rd., Monterey

Apex Rent-A-Car of Monterey, 2555 Garden Rd. or Hilton Inn, 1000 Aguajito Rd., Monterey

Avis Rent A Car, Monterey Peninsula Airport or Ocean Ave. & Fremont, Monterey; Carmel Holiday Inn, Hwy. 1 & Rio Rd., Carmel

Budget Rent A Car, Fairgrounds Travelodge, 2030A Fremont, Monterey

Dollar Rent-A-Car System, Don Lucas Ford, Washington & E. Franklin, Monterey

Hertz Rent A Car, Monterey Peninsula Airport or Del Monte

Hyatt House, 1 Old Golf Course Rd., Monterey; The Lodge at Pebble Beach; Quail Lodge, Carmel Valley Rd., Carmel Valley.

Merry Rent-a-Car, 3 Heitzinger Plaza, Seaside

National Car Rental, Monterey Peninsula Airport, Monterey

Sears Rent A Car, Fairgrounds Travelodge, 2030A Fremont, Monterey

Thrifty Rent-A-Car, Monterey Holiday Inn, 2600 Sand Dunes Rd., Monterey

BICYCLE RENTALS

Bicycles-by-the-Sea, Beachcomber Inn, 1996 Sunset Dr., Pacific Grove. Available every day.

Freewheeling Cycles, 188 Webster St., Monterey. Open every day.

Les Joselyn Bicycles, 638 Lighthouse Ave., Monterey. Closed Sundays and Mondays.

Valley Auto Supply & Cyclery, 538 Carmel Rancho Shopping Ctr., Carmel. Closed Sundays.

BUS AND LIMOUSINE TOURS

GRAY LINE OF MONTEREY–CARMEL, Casa Munras Garden Hotel, Monterey, has a tour of Monterey and Carmel, 25 miles, about 2½ hours, including Monterey's historic adobes, Cannery Row, Pacific Grove's shoreline, Seventeen-Mile Drive, Carmel, and Carmel Mission Basilica. This tour leaves at 1:30 P.M. Monday, Wednesday, and Friday from June through September. Gray Line also has a tour from Monterey to Hearst Castle at San Simeon from June through September.

CHARTERED LIMOUSINE SERVICE, INC., Carmel, offers chauffeur-driven sightseeing tours for small or large groups, including after-dark night-life tours. Reservations necessary. Twenty-four-hour passenger service to and from all airports is also available.

JOE'S TAXI, Mission & 8th, Carmel, provides guided scenic tours of Seventeen-Mile Drive and historic points of interest for small parties. Call for information.

MONTEREY PENINSULA TRANSIT routes extend throughout the Peninsula and serve many points of interest. A system map appears at the front of the Yellow Pages of the telephone book, and complete schedules are available from drivers. The exact fare is 35¢ with free transfer privileges. Trips through Fort Ord to Salinas leave hourly from downtown Monterey, Tyler and Franklin Sts.

BIG SUR GETAWAY, Bus No. 22, is the title of Monterey Peninsula Transit's two round trips daily between Monterey/Carmel and Big Sur during summer months. Stops are made at various locations along Highway 1, such as Carmel Highlands, Point Lobos, and Pfeiffer Big Sur State Park. The ride takes about 1½ hours each way. Buses leave downtown Monterey at 10 A.M. and 1 P.M. Return trips leave Nepenthe at 11:30 A.M. and 2:30 P.M.

BOAT EXCURSIONS

SAM'S FISHING FLEET, Fisherman's Wharf, Monterey, offers 45-minute cruises around Monterey Bay. Boats operate year-round, daily during summer months and weekends only during the rest of the year. Reservations are requested. During winter months Sam's Fishing Fleet also has whale-watching cruises so you can see migrating whales as they swim past the entrance to Monterey Bay.

FRANK'S FISHING TRIPS, Fisherman's Wharf, Monterey, has a similar but shorter bay cruise (30 minutes). No reservations are required.

CHRIS' FISHING TRIPS and BENJI'S FISHING TRIPS, both at Fisherman's Wharf, Monterey, also offer bay cruises.

GLASS-BOTTOMED BOAT TOURS around Lovers Point, Pacific Grove, to view underwater marine life last 30 minutes. This tour is offered during the summer only.

BOAT RENTALS

El Estero Boating, Lake El Estero, Monterey. Pedal boats and canoes for paddling around the lake. Open daily 10:30 A.M. –5 P.M.

Pacific Grove Boat Rentals, 626 Ocean View Blvd., Pacific Grove. Pedal boats, kayaks, rowboats and motor boats. Open daily 6 A.M.–6 P.M. Memorial Day through Labor Day. Reservations accepted.

Monterey Bay Yacht Center, Wharf No. 2, Monterey. Yacht rentals only.

FISHING TRIPS

CHRIS', FRANK'S, RANDY'S, SAM'S and BENJI'S, all on Fisherman's Wharf, Monterey, provide daily fishing trips. Rates vary. Rods can be rented; bait is free with rental. Dress warmly and don't forget to pack a lunch and take along a thermos with a hot drink.

A three-day fishing license costs $2. and can be obtained on Fisherman's Wharf. If you plan to return to fish again, an annual license at $4. is a better buy. Youngsters under 16 do not need licenses. Free licenses for persons over 65 are available from the California State Department of Fish & Game, 2301 Garden Rd., Monterey.

HORSES FOR HIRE

Double-A Stable, 550 Aguajito Rd., Monterey. Open daily at 9:30 A.M. except Monday.

Pebble Beach Equestrian Center, Portola Rd., Pebble Beach. Reservations required. Open daily.

Carmel Valley Riding & Polo Center, Robinson Canyon Rd., Carmel Valley. Escorted trail rides. Reservations required. Open Tuesday-Saturday.

BIG SUR

Big Sur Campgrounds. May 1–Sept. 30 only.
Fernwood
Limekiln Beach Redwoods
Pfeiffer Big Sur State Park
Riverside Campgrounds. May 25–Sept. 25 only.
Ventana Campgrounds
The U.S. Forest Service has several campgrounds south of Big Sur village. Information can be obtained at the Big Sur Guard Station just south of the entrance to Pfeiffer Big Sur State Park.

CARMEL VALLEY

Riverside Park, Schulte Rd.
Saddle Mountain Recreation Park, Schulte Rd.
Information about campgrounds in Los Padres National Forest is available at the Ranger Station at Los Padres Dam.

MONTEREY

Monterey Peninsula College, Parking Lot C, 980 Fremont St.
    Weekends during August only.
Veterans Memorial Park (municipal), top of Jefferson St.

MOSS LANDING

KOA Kampgrounds of America, 338 Giberson Rd.

PACIFIC GROVE

17 Mile Drive Village, 17 Mile Dr. and Sinex Ave.

Green Parrot Mobile Park, 835 Kimball Ave.
Trailer Terrace, 1206 La Salle Ave.

SKINDIVING AND SCUBA EQUIPMENT RENTALS

Aquarius Dive Shop, 2240 Del Monte Ave., Monterey. Open
every day.
Ed Brawley's Skin Diving School, 598 Foam St., Monterey.
Open every day.
Monterey Dive Center, 763 Lighthouse Ave., Monterey. Open
every day.

12.
Year-Round
Extraspecial Events

JANUARY

Monterey Co. Symphony Assn. Concert Series – Monterey
   Peninsula College, Monterey and Sunset Center, Carmel
Monterey Peninsula Chamber Music Soc. Concert Series –
   Sunset Center, Carmel
Great Plays on Film – Sunset Center, Carmel
Bing Crosby Natl. Pro-Amateur Golf Championship, 4 days –
   Pebble Beach
Championship Cat Show, 2 days – Monterey Co. Fairgrounds,
   Monterey

FEBRUARY

Classic Guitar Festival, 2 days – Sunset Center, Carmel
Carmel Music Soc. Concert Series – Sunset Center, Carmel
Monterey Co. Symphony Assn. Concert Series – Monterey
   Peninsula College, Monterey and Sunset Center, Carmel
Monterey Peninsula Chamber Music Soc. Concert Series –
   Sunset Center, Carmel
Opera Ensemble – Hidden Valley Theatre, Carmel Valley
Festival of Dance – Sunset Center, Carmel
Great Plays on Film – Sunset Center, Carmel
Creative Needlework Show, 1 week – Monterey Peninsula
   Museum of Art, Monterey

The Beacon House, one of the homes on Victorian   *143*
Home Tour

Cascarone Ball – Del Monte Hyatt House, Monterey
Monterey Co. Painting Competition – Monterey Peninsula
    Museum of Art, Monterey
Backgammon Championship, 2 days – The Lodge at Pebble
    Beach

MARCH

Good Old Days, 1 week – Pacific Grove
Victorian House Tour – Pacific Grove
Carmel Music Soc. Concert Series – Sunset Center, Carmel
Monterey Co. Symphony Assn. Concert Series – Monterey
    Peninsula College, Monterey and Sunset Center, Carmel
Monterey Peninsula Chamber Music Soc. Concert Series –
    Sunset Center, Carmel
Opera Ensemble – Hidden Valley Theatre, Carmel Valley
Great Plays on Film – Sunset Center, Carmel
Festival of Dance – Sunset Center, Carmel
Karkapades, 3 days – Monterey Co. Fairgrounds, Monterey
Ano Nuevo Race – Monterey Peninsula Yacht Club, Monterey
Natl. Rugby Championship, 2 days – Collins Field, Pebble
    Beach
Spring Horse Show – Carmel Valley Trail & Saddle Club
Winter Horse Show – Pebble Beach Equestrian Center

APRIL

Adobe Tour, 2 days – Monterey
Kite Flying Contest – Carmel
Kids' Day – Los Arboles School, Marina
Carmel Music Soc. Concert Series – Sunset Center, Carmel
Monterey Peninsula Chamber Music Soc. Concert Series –
    Sunset Center, Carmel
Monterey Peninsula Choral Soc. Concert Series – Monterey
    Peninsula College, Monterey and Sunset Center, Carmel

Great Plays on Film – Sunset Center, Carmel
Wild Flower Show, 3 days – Pacific Grove Museum of Natural History
Aviation Exposition, 3 days – Monterey Peninsula Airport, Monterey
Butterfly Criterium (bicycle races) – Pacific Grove
Sports Car Races – Laguna Seca Raceway, Monterey
Calif. State Open Tennis Championship – Beach & Tennis Club, Pebble Beach
Easter Seal Golf Tournament – Spyglass Hill Golf Course, Pebble Beach
Senior Invitational Golf Tournament, 4 days – Monterey Peninsula Country Club, Pebble Beach
Polo Matches – Collins Field, Pebble Beach
Hunt Race Meet & Steeplechase – Pebble Beach Equestrian Center
Moss Landing Marine Laboratories' Open House – Moss Landing
Fiesta de Los Amigos – Carmel Valley

MAY

Garden Tour – Monterey Peninsula Volunteer Services
Home Show, 5 days – Monterey Co. Fairgrounds, Monterey
Antique Show, 2 days – Monterey Co. Fairgrounds, Monterey
Armed Forces Day – Fort Ord
Defense Language Institute Open House – Presidio, Monterey
Monterey Co. Symphony Assn. Concert Series – Monterey Peninsula College, Monterey and Sunset Center, Carmel
Monterey Co. Symphony Pops Concert – Monterey Co. Fairgrounds, Monterey
Monterey Peninsula Chamber Music Soc. Concert Series – Sunset Center, Carmel
Monterey Peninsula Choral Soc. Concert Series – Sunset Center, Carmel
Opera Ensemble – Hidden Valley Theatre, Carmel Valley

Great Plays on Film – Sunset Center, Carmel

Bonsai Show, 2 days – Monterey Peninsula Buddhist Temple, Seaside

Scale Model Show – Pacific Grove

Sports Car Races – Laguna Seca Raceway, Monterey

Motorcycle Races – Monterey Co. Fairgrounds, Monterey

Sailboat Races – Monterey Peninsula Yacht Club, Monterey

Commodore's Regatta, 2 days – Stillwater Yacht Club, Pebble Beach

Shark Derby – Moss Landing

Calif. State Fish and Game Mariculture Laboratory Open House – Granite Canyon, Big Sur

Pony Club Horse Show – Pebble Beach Equestrian Center

Hunter Trials – Collins Field, Pebble Beach

Del Monte Kennel Club Dog Show – Collins Field, Pebble Beach

Cat Fanciers Show, 2 days – Monterey Co. Fairgrounds, Monterey

JUNE

Merienda (Monterey's birthday celebration) – Memory Garden, Monterey

Fiesta de Los Padres – San Carlos Cathedral, Monterey

Week of the Bayonet, 5 days – Fort Ord

Monterey Co. Symphony Assn. Concert Series – Monterey Peninsula College, Monterey and Sunset Center, Carmel

Monterey Peninsula Choral Soc. Concerts, 2 days – Carmel Mission Basilica

Great Plays on Film – Sunset Center, Carmel

Coin Show, 2 days – Monterey Peninsula Coin Club

Arts & Crafts Fair, 2 days – Custom House Plaza, Monterey

Monterey City Women's Golf Tournament, 6 days – Old Del Monte Golf Course, Monterey

Sports Car Races – Laguna Seca Raceway, Monterey

Antique, Classic & Vintage Car Show – Pacific Grove

Motorcycle Races – Monterey Co. Fairgrounds, Monterey
Sailboat Races – Monterey Peninsula Yacht Club, Monterey
Stuart Haldorn Regatta – Stillwater Yacht Club, Pebble Beach
Morgan Horse Show, 3 days – Monterey Co. Fairgrounds,
　Monterey
Shark Derby – Moss Landing

JULY

Fourth of July Parade – Seaside
Fourth of July Fireworks Display – Coast Guard Pier,
　Monterey
Sloat Landing Re-Enactment – Custom House Plaza,
　Monterey
Obon Festival, 2 days – Monterey Co. Fairgrounds, Monterey
Feast of Lanterns, 1 week – Pacific Grove
Espiritu Santos Portuguese Festival, 2 days – Portuguese Hall,
　Monterey
Community Fair, 2 days – Del Monte Shopping Center,
　Monterey
Flea Market & Festival – Moss Landing
Bach Festival, 2 weeks – Sunset Center, Carmel
Summer Sunday Afternoon Concert Series – Forest Theater,
　Carmel
Shakespearean Festival – Forest Theater, Carmel
Antique Show & Sale, 2 days – St. Mary's-by-the-Sea
　Episcopal Church, Pacific Grove
Water Color Show – Pacific Grove Art Center
Indian Art Show & Sale, 3 days – Monterey Co. Fairgrounds,
　Monterey
Arts & Crafts Fair, 2 days – Custom House Plaza, Monterey
Motorcycle Races, 2 days – Laguna Seca Raceway, Monterey
Bicycle Classic – Collins Field, Pebble Beach
Mixed Foursome Tournament – Pacific Grove Municipal Golf
　Links

Peter Hay, Jr. Golf Championship, 4 days – Peter Hay Golf
Course, Pebble Beach
Seniors Tennis Tournament – Pacific Grove Municipal Tennis
Courts
Matthew C. Jenkins Regatta, 2 days – Stillwater Yacht Club,
Pebble Beach
Sailboat Races – Monterey Peninsula Yacht Club, Monterey
Morgan Horse Show, 2 days – Monterey Co.. Fairgrounds,
Monterey
Natl. Horse Show, 5 days – Monterey Co. Fairgrounds,
Monterey

AUGUST

Monterey Co. Fair, 6 days – Monterey Co. Fairgrounds,
Monterey
Festival & Fish Fry – Moss Landing
Hidden Valley Seminars Concert Series – Hidden Valley
Theatre, Carmel Valley
Summer Sunday Afternoon Concert Series – Forest Theater,
Carmel
Shakespearean Festival – Forest Theater, Carmel
Arts & Crafts Fair, 2 days – Custom House Plaza, Monterey
Scottish Highland Games – Collins Field, Pebble Beach
Concours d'Elégance (classic car show) – The Lodge at Pebble
Beach
Historic Automobile Races – Laguna Seca Raceway,
Monterey
Woman's Golf Invitational, 3 days – Monterey Peninsula
Country Club, Pebble Beach
Sailboat Races – Monterey Peninsula Yacht Club, Monterey
Corridos de Toros Sailboat Races – Stillwater Yacht Club,
Pebble Beach
Arabian Horse Show, 2 days – Monterey Co. Fairgrounds,
Monterey
Natl. Horse Show, 5 days – Monterey Co. Fairgrounds,
Monterey

Dressage Championship, 2 days—Pebble Beach Equestrian
  Center
Three-Day Equestrian Event—Pebble Beach Equestrian
  Center
All Breed Shorthair Cat Show—Monterey Co. Fairgrounds,
  Monterey

SEPTEMBER

House Tour—Women's Architectural League
Santa Rosalia Festival—Custom House Plaza and Fisherman's
  Wharf, Monterey
Black Observance, 3 days—Seaside and Monterey Co.
  Fairgrounds, Monterey
Artichoke Festival, 2 days—Castroville
Carmel Mission Fiesta—Carmel Mission Basilica
Monterey Jazz Festival, 3 days—Monterey Co. Fairgrounds,
  Monterey
Great Plays on Film—Sunset Center, Carmel
Antique Show & Sale, 3 days—Monterey Conference Center
Water Color Show—Pacific Grove Museum of Natural History
Quilt Show, 3 days—Chautauqua Hall, Pacific Grove

Concours d'Elegance

Gem & Mineral Show, 2 days – Monterey Co. Fairgrounds, Monterey
Motorcycle Races – Laguna Seca Raceway, Monterey
Hole-in-One Contest, 2 days – Pacific Grove Municipal Golf Links
Vintage Tennis Tournament, 1 week – Beach & Tennis Club, Pebble Beach
Labor Day Invitational Regatta, 2 days – Stillwater Yacht Club, Pebble Beach
Outrigger Regatta, 2 days – Monterey Peninsula Yacht Club, Monterey
Animal Faire – Custom House Plaza, Monterey
Equestrian Trials, 3 days – Pebble Beach Equestrian Center
Fort Ord Riding Club Fall Review, 2 days – Fort Ord
Arabian Horse Show, 2 days – Monterey Co. Fairgrounds, Monterey

OCTOBER

Great Sand Castle Contest – Carmel Beach
Butterfly Parade & Bazaar – Pacific Grove
Military Appreciation Week – All Cities
Hallowe'en Parade & Party – Moss Landing
Pumpkin Carving Contest – Carmel
Pumpkin Carving & Decorating Contest – Del Monte Hyatt House, Monterey
Carmel Music Soc. Concert Series – Monterey Peninsula College, Monterey and Sunset Center, Carmel
Monterey Co. Symphony Assn. Concert Series – Monterey Peninsula College, Monterey and Sunset Center, Carmel
Monterey Peninsula Chamber Music Soc. Concert Series – Sunset Center, Carmel
Folk Festival, 2 days – Monterey Peninsula College, Monterey
Great Plays on Film – Sunset Center, Carmel
Festival of Dance – Sunset Center, Carmel
Kaleidoscope, 2 days – Monterey Co. Fairgrounds, Monterey

Monterey Grand Prix Formula 5000, 3 days – Laguna Seca
Raceway, Monterey
Sailboat Races – Monterey Peninsula Yacht Club, Monterey
Social Spectator Polo, 3 days – Collins Field, Pebble Beach
Wine Stomp – Monterey Winery, Monterey

NOVEMBER

Winter Parade – Pacific Grove
Table Fashion Show – Carmel
Community Thanksgiving Potluck Dinner – Monterey Co.
Fairgrounds, Monterey
Carmel Music Soc. Concert Series – Sunset Center, Carmel
Monterey Co. Symphony Assn. Concert Series – Monterey
Peninsula College, Monterey and Sunset Center, Carmel
Monterey Peninsula Chamber Music Soc. Concert Series –
Sunset Center, Carmel
Great Plays on Film – Sunset Center, Carmel
Festival of Dance – Sunset Center, Carmel
Competitive Art Exhibition – Seaside City Hall
Homecrafters' Marketplace – Sunset Center, Carmel
Celebrity Golf Tournament – Rancho Cañada Golf & Country
Club, Carmel Valley
Sailboat Races – Monterey Peninsula Yacht Club, Monterey
Golden Domino Tournament – Monterey Peninsula Country
Club, Pebble Beach
Backgammon Tournament – The Lodge at Pebble Beach

DECEMBER

Calif. Wine Festival, Monterey Peninsula Seminar on Fine
Wines, 4 days – Major Hotels and Monterey Conference
Center
Filipino Maria Clara Festival – Monterey Co. Fairgrounds,
Monterey

Festival of the Trees, 5 days – Monterey Co. Fairgrounds, Monterey

Christmas-by-the-Sea, 2 days – La Playa Hotel, Carmel

39 Craftsmen Bring Christmas, 2 days – La Playa Hotel, Carmel

Renaissance Faire, 3 days – Carmel Center

Christmas Pageant, 3 evenings – First Church of God, Pacific Grove

Singing Christmas Tree, 3 evenings – Assembly of God Church, Pacific Grove

Residential Christmas Tour – Pacific Grove

Music for Christmas – Carmel Mission Basilica

Community Christmas Potluck Dinner – Monterey Co. Fairgrounds, Monterey

Jewish Festival – Old Oak Grove School, Monterey

Great Plays on Film – Sunset Center, Carmel

Cam Puget Golf Tournament – Pebble Beach Golf Links

Sailboat Races – Monterey Peninsula Yacht Club, Monterey

Del Monte Kennel Club All-Breed Match – Monterey Co. Fairgrounds, Monterey

Index

157

ABOUT THE AUTHORS

A transplanted Washingtonian, **Maxine Knox**, since moving to the Monterey Peninsula many years ago, has done newspaper advertising and business promotion for hotels and restaurants. She and her family live in Pacific Grove.

As the wife of a Navy Commander, **Mary Rodriguez**, lived in many places, but on her husband's retirement Monterey became their permanent home. Mary is a columnist for the *Monterey Peninsula Herald* and a staff writer on *This Month Magazine*.

A mutual hobby, contesting—at which they were very successful—brought Maxine and Mary together and their friendship grew into a writing team, at which they are equally successful. This book is their third team effort.